here among the gods
you know all is all
there is no this or that
only all

everything is known
because nothing is apart
there is no alone or together
only all
just as water fills the basin
so your soul fills the heavens

time does not exist
there is no now then or when
because all is all
time knowledge people birds trees memory life
everything is here for you
and there as well
you need only release the self-imposed chains
that bind your soul

let go of doubt, know no fear
because all is all
uncertainty resides with certainty
pain is pleasure's brother
there is no you to feel the pain that does not exist
you have attempted to remove yourself from the pool
but it is impossible
even in your delusion you are but a part of all
you needn't try

there are no gods
because all is all
in your error you deify that which you see as outside yourself
but all is all
the light you see as god is you
the eyelids you cower behind are you
you are all because all is all

thunder that never ends, only resonates in motion
rain that neither falls nor dries, only moves
a birds wing, the mite on its skin
the parasitic bacteria on the mite
the brief flickers of focused energy that make up the cells
and the vast font of energy that keeps them in proximity
all is all

you cannot separate yourself
either physically or in spirit
you cannot segment your mind
from the mind of god
just as your soul is but one breath
so your mind is but one spark
but the breath and the spark are all

there is no telepathy
because there is no separation of our minds
there is no fortune telling
because it's all happening right now
time is an illusion you have attempted to create
but your actions of yesterday
are your actions of tomorrow
because all is all
it's all there, it's all done

I cannot touch you
there is no you or I or we or they
because all is all
there is no enemy or lover
there is no pen or foot or wooden floor
it is all, because all is all

the separation you imagine is an illusion
the chair is the tree
the poison is the river
the air is the rock
the known is the unknown

the truth a lie and the lie a truth
because all is all
same pool without limits
no scope or boundaries

the concept of size and scale and relativity
are simply part of your illusion,
your attempt to rationalize your separation

by working to define that which you see as outside yourself,
you prolong the illusion of being outside of it
but even your illusion is a part of it
because all is all
the entirety of the universe
resides within the space of an atom
because the atom is the universe
and the universe the atom

there is was or never will be a creation
for that would imply an end to come
not a creator
for that would imply the created
but all is all
the beginning and the end
the creator and the created
you are not a father
for you are not separate from your daughter
but all is all
we are they
she is you
he is was and will be

do not seek the god you have imagined
for one is not hidden from the other
but all is all
we they dog tree ice rain music
all is all

you can neither come nor go
it's all the same
it's not over
because it never began
it simply is

there are no friends or strangers,
no conversations to be missed
no sane or insane,
drunkenness or sobriety
no leaders or followers,
crime or punishment
these are but illusory distinctions
of flickering fragments of all

there is no need to commit this to memory
for there is nothing to learn or to forget
the energy of the sun
is the energy of your thoughts
the sensation of the breeze
is the sensation of your touch

there is no black or white,
exciting or boring
no beautiful or ugly,
ignorant or brilliant
no creative or non
poetic or mute

all is all
and all is good
for all is all there is

# In Search of a New Millennium

## Twentieth Anniversary Edition

One Man's Quest For The 21st Century, Along The Road To Peace, Understanding, Purpose, and Destiny

by Aaron James

Dedicated to my daughter, who first taught me the beauty of the Inner Child.

And to Superman, in hopes that the ideals of Truth, Justice, and the American Way, never die.

And to Saint Jane.

© 2020  Aaron James
All rights reserved

ISBN: 9798640704310

Independently published using
Kindle Direct Publishing by Amazon

Opening poem: *Here Among the Gods* is a stream of consciousness piece written early one morning in the summer of '99, at a lovely little coffee shop in the Marigny district of New Orleans.

Front cover illustration: The original vision sketch of a built environment for 200 years hence, which I call MegaCity. For an idea of the scale, each gridline equals fifty feet (note the "normal" sized buildings underneath.)

Back cover illustration: A self-designed tattoo that describes my religion. The sun represents Nature, Universal Energy, and the Golden Orb. Yen/Yang acknowledges the Eastern portions of my beliefs, the Greek cross the Western. "T-A-H-C-D" stands for: "Thought-Act-Habit-Character-Destiny", meaning your thoughts are the primary determinant of your destiny, which, in a nutshell, could be construed as the Humanist portion of my beliefs.

Back cover photo by Jamie Harmon of Memphis

# Introduction

Knowledge is an accumulation of understanding, a system of beliefs, and a standard of truths. Some would argue that we understand so little about ourselves and the Universe that not only can we assume no Truths, but that science itself is merely a continuous process of proving itself wrong. The flaw in this thinking is that to reject knowledge is to invite insanity. Human knowledge is a *progression* of truths, but we must maintain a firm grasp on what we know while groping for what we do not. What follows is my attempt at sharing a few things I think I know, while simultaneously seeking the unknown. It is by no means intended to resemble the All Knowing, for to claim "all knowing" is to proclaim ultimate ignorance.

It is true that much of the lacking I see in the world, I also see in myself. That the glory I hope for mankind, I also hope for myself. And the longing for something only imagined, is only imagined of myself as well. To want is to dream. To dream is to live in a time and place that as yet does not exist. What else is worthy of our dreams but beauty, joy, and passion? It is these things I crave for myself. I pray for the strength to consistently seek these within myself. A future of any less brilliance would not be of sufficient enticement to call me forward. Man deserves to walk on streets of gold, but if this is true for any of us, it is true for all of us. We are not a thread but a fabric, and the pattern we weave is of our own design. I see a better world for us all, I *crave* a better world for us all. Somewhere within the depths of your soul you feel the same. Only together can we bring about the future we deserve.

Sometime during the winter of '99-'00, I had a vision of a built environment for 200 years hence, which I call MegaCity: A gigantic, self-contained and self-sufficient cube designed to provide living and work space for one million people. In order to put yourself in the right mindset, imagine you are an architect living in 1773. One day an image comes to you of two soaring towers of some strange, svelte design, like nothing you've ever seen. Even though you have no clue as to what it's all about, you make a quick sketch and try to describe it as best you can. The problem is the technology required for its construction, function, and use, are all completely outside your present realm of comprehension. Then 200 years later, some inquisitive architectural student rediscovers your work and is flabbergasted to discover that the supposedly inexplicable building concept you had struggled with was what he now knows as the World Trade Center. The concept of such an environment not only led to a consideration of the social changes required to make such a facility function, but of how we, as a species, might actually manage to survive long enough to make it happen.

I should warn you there's not much about this book to keep you glued to the pages like a Tom Clancy novel or some such. I will go so far as to admit it is little more than the self-righteous ramblings of a delusional egoist, whose main justification in life is to seek drama and adventure where none exists, meaning where there probably is none, and some goddamn sense of purpose, when in fact even this has been proven to be a mere ploy of the ego. He expresses so much disappointment with his fellow humans and their self-imposed stations in life that it's all but impossible to see through this dank fog to determine if there may actually be anything of substance underneath.

Yes, I try to imagine there is some meaning and purpose to life, and therefore some meaning and purpose to my own, and generally seek motivations to help substantiate this belief. Yes, I am extremely disappointed with much of what I see around me, but mainly because there is so much untapped potential in all of us that it's impossible for me to just sit idly by and watch the fires of humanity die. And *you*, my friend, are humanity. As am I. And that is why I'm not concerned about contemporary society's misunderstandings about the ego, because the ego is by definition the self. And the self, as far as you are aware, is all there is. And if you can't celebrate your own existence, then it's impossible for you to find joy in anything. The only bad ego is a false ego. Like the shallow bastard who spends 20 minutes every morning blow drying his hair because he has attached so much of his self-image to the dead protein cells sprouting off the top of his hollow skull.

Why am I getting into this now? I have no idea really. Notions fly thru my head all the time. Sometimes they snag a bit of gray matter on the way out and I feel I have to chase them down. I was just concerned about the fact there is little of entertainment value to the pages that follow. In the end, I suppose there's a fine line between self-awareness and self-deceit. All I can do is ask you to read on, judge every word on your own, and forgive me on the occasions when I cross that line. What follows is as real and open and honest as I can get. Is part of it boring? Of course. Are there any kernels of Truth that may get stuck in your teeth? Let me just say I sincerely hope so, because if not, this entire effort has been one gigantic waste of time.

# Quick Reference Guide to Character Identifiers

Obviously I do not use real names and instead assigned most characters a simple two or three letter identifier. Here is the list, in the order they appear in the book.

| | |
|---|---|
| AO: | Stepmother |
| KB: | Friend I met at King Biscuit Blues Festival |
| JR: | Oldest brother |
| DAB: | Middle brother |
| SJ: | Saint Jane |
| OB: | Nephew, my oldest brother's son |
| CL | Daughter |
| BBF: | Brilliant biologist friend |
| PF: | Friend I met on South Padre', Padre' Fred |

## Monday August 21st 2000

The real problem is while we're off living drama in our heads, the world around us is dieing. Within ourselves, our muscles die and our heart dies, as do our hopes, dreams, and ambitions. I look around and see so much death, so much loneliness and unhappiness. What death do others, with a greater capacity than my own, see in me? What can I be doing right here on this bus to bring more life to those around me? Should I stand and preach? Lead a mini-revival or group sing-along?

Instead I sit stone-faced and quiet like all the others. The only difference is I am playing out my drama by moving an ink stick across a page. I long for the time, 6-8 weeks hence, when I can sleep all day under a tree. There I will find myself. There I will rid myself of my accumulated death. Then I will live. Then I will be able to preach and rambunctiously lead a group sing-along. And the life spark in those around me will recognize the fire in my eyes and they will Know. For now I remain partly shrouded in death…

But I have a plan.

# ❧ Book I ❧

*Thursday October 26th 2000*

Sitting at the Map Room, my funky neighborhood coffee bar, trying to figure out why the hell I can't get out of this town. I would start at the beginning and tell you what this new journal is all about but right now I'm not in the mood. I'm frustrated with my truck, despise my family, and hate Memphis!

Okay, enough attitude.

Most people spend a large portion of their lives trying to relate to their parents. For me they are one of the main reasons why I have to go. I've come to appreciate the fact that my childhood could have been much worse. Fortunately, being the baby, my siblings absorbed most of the beatings. I have a picture of myself on my 4th birthday but find it nearly impossible to relate to the image. One of these days however, I will meet this little boy and listen intently to what he has to say about myself and this thing we call life.

God, I'm not in the mood to write. I guess I chose a bad time to pick up a pen, but I had to start sometime. I'm halfway through my 37th year, which bears no direct significance except to gauge the distance I've traveled so far. If things go as planned, this will be a journal of my long anticipated trek around the country. Like many others before me, I have always had a burning desire to just chuck it all and travel.

## Sunday October 29th 2000

Map Room again, listening to the Beatles. I've done absolutely squat all weekend but hole-up and watch videos. I've come to detest factual journal entries but I suppose it would help you to know what's going on. Friday, I...

Wait. I have to catch you up on the important things first. Regarding the above entry, you will find...

Wait. If I just come right out and say my writing fluctuates with my mood, then I blow any chance of you discovering this part of my stylistic genius on your own. But unfortunately my writing *does* fluctuate with my mood, which is why I'm torn between forcing myself to write every day or only attempting to capture the good stuff. But since this is a real time journal of an adventure, I have no way of knowing when to expect the good stuff and therefore when to whip out the journal. And about the false starts, I don't like it when my writing turns cheesy or forced or down the wrong track, so I just stop. The best writing comes from the pen simply moving across the page. Sometimes even I am amazed at the result.

And now, back to our story...

My father is probably the dumbest SOB I've ever known. What's worse, he's not just dumb in the unlearned, under-stimulated sense of the word, but in the inconceivable, intentional sense. It's like he wears his ignorance like a crown, except for when he tucks his crown under his arm to use as a crutch. Anyway, the other day he finally did something halfway intelligent. Friday I gave up on fixing my truck (a 1962 Ford F100) by myself and decided to tow it to my high school sweetheart's parents' garage. So my father calls his insurance company and tells them it's *his* truck that's broken down, then gets the tow driver to jimmy the paperwork and pull my truck instead - brilliant!

The story of my high school sweetheart is a book unto itself. My first real meaningful love was a beautiful and beautifully sweet sophomore. We dated for just over two years and while most of it was incredible, we were ultimately torn apart by the misguided passions of youth. But her family was good to me. Her father owned a garage and would let me come in and tinker. I went over there a couple of weeks ago to get advice on a good head shop and I swear not a single thing had changed in eighteen years. But my sweetheart's mother told me she is now a crack addicted prostitute somewhere on Summer Avenue. I tried a few times to drive around looking for her, but with no luck.

*Monday October 30th Y2K 7:30 AM*

I'm sitting outside my stepmother's (AO) hospital room, listening to some nurse talk to her like a child. Christmas of '96 the doctors gave her three months to live and she's been existing in various states of health ever since. I knew when I decided to leave I would probably miss her funeral, and in fact still hope I do. Not that I'm cold to the reality, it's just I've already accepted it. Now the nurse is asking, "Do you know where you are?" and, "When's your birthday?" This is a woman who used to arm wrestle my fraternity brothers whenever I'd throw a party. She's also the main reason I was able to maintain sanity through my teen years, although technically she only had to physically intervene between my father and I once.

A nurse came by and made me get off the floor. She put me in a chair where I can now see AO lying in her bed. Have you ever watched a premature puppy die, all jittery and disoriented? If this is why the Gods made me stay in town over the weekend, let me now say, "Okay, I get it, let me go." I know she would. But that's why I stayed holed-up, I knew destiny was playing some kind of trick on me and I wanted to avoid all possibility of finding out what. One scary thing is I could almost swear I had read yesterday's paper's cover story a few months ago. It's such moments of déjà vu that clue me into glimpses through the portal. I do not believe in predetermined fate, but I definitely believe we are each responsible for being aware of, and reacting to, those fragmentary moments that could change our lives, even if we fail to notice or react to them.

*same day 11:00 AM*

I finally got to see AO for a few minutes. It's funny but she seemed fairly coherent when I was there, but then my dad came in and started with the baby talk and she drifted away again. Now I'm facing dealing with my family for not wanting to wait around for her funeral, which may or may not be imminent. I've already said my goodbyes, I want to go!

I got my truck running, sort of. Good enough to get across the bridge anyway. At this point that's all I care about. I would much rather be broken down in the middle of nowhere than here. At least then I would be forced to deal with it on my own, or at least more directly gauge and deal with the benevolence of others, rather than fall back on my old patterns of reliance. I've been having romantic notions of working in a diner in some small town and doing little else for the next few months except working on the truck. But it's no great secret that major portions of my life are spent entertaining romantic notions. I mean let's face it, this entire adventure is nothing but one gigantic romantic notion. Only while dealing with any one particular portion of it, will it ever be anything but.

That makes twice today I've avoided opportunities to elaborate on partially expressed ideas. For instance, I could go on for days about my romantic notions of practically everything. I'm rarely able to look at anything without seeing a better version of it. Plus, my notions of man have little to do with weakness or socially fabricated frailties. Again I could go on, but I'm just not in the mood. Give me a few days away from this hellhole and I'll try to fill in the blanks.

## Tuesday October 31st Y2K

We made it across the bridge! The truck was churning and jostling so much I felt like Orville Wright at Kitty Hawk, but we pulled off at the first exit and are two-lane'ing it from here.

*same day 9:27 PM*

I'm on my way to Springfield, Missouri, to hang out a couple of days with a friend I met at King Biscuit Blues Festival in Helena, Arkansas (so we'll call her KB.) I'm now parked under the Highway 64 bridge on the good side of the White River. If today is any indication as to what to expect of my adventure, I should do okay. When I first got to Marion, Arkansas, I spent an hour driving around looking for a junkyard, but soon realized I was trying too hard and decided to just head on down the road. I needed to scavenge a little metal ring that helps gasket the exhaust manifold to the head. It wasn't twenty minutes later that I saw a junkyard about a 1/4 mile off the road to the right. So I pulled in and asked the owner if he had any early '60 Ford pickups. He sent me to one that turned out to have the wrong size engine, but he said I could pull the manifold anyway to see if it had the part I needed, which it didn't. So he fished around in his shop and came up with a metal ring camshaft bushing, *then* let me use his tools to alter it to fit my manifold, *and* didn't charge me a GD penny for any of it! (He's a "church goin' man" and doesn't like it when people say goddamn.) Is that cool or what?! There I was, happy as a GD lark, grinding and cutting and hammering on this GD metal ring, and I swear to god, the fucking thing **fit**! I was in low budget, road travelin', hog freakin' heaven. He kept making comments like, "We Hill-billies can teach you city fellas a thing or two about making do."

All in all it was an excellent experience. As I was about to drive off he gave me a fried chicken and potato kabob he had gotten from the local Quick Stop. He said he goes by there every morning and buys what they have left over from the day before. "Whatever we don't eat, we feed to the dogs." I guess I fell somewhere in between. If you've never tried chicken and potato kabobs from a southern Quick Stop, infrared-all-day buffet, then... Well, I won't say you don't know what you're missing, but if you go to New York just for the vendor dogs, then you know what I mean.

### Thursday November 2nd 2000 6:00 AM

I'm in the heart of the Ozarks, otherwise known as Calico Rock, Arkansas, at the White River Café: 2 eggs with hash browns, biscuits, and gravy for $2.10. This is the land for me by god. (I keep trying to whistle *Dueling Banjos* but it keeps coming out as *Popcorn*.)

It's occurred to me I won't be able to share all of the details of my trip. To put it dramatically, "My world is awash with detail." The hills are beautiful with fog and colored leaves. A white rabbit ran across my headlights on the way in this morning. Last night (that's yesterday afternoon to those who function after sundown) I saw a huge spider walking across the road. I drove by a beautiful swimming hole carved into a natural rock hillside. My brakes are virtually non-existent and pull hard right... Tons and tons of cool little things like that.

Anyway, Wednesday morning I left my spot under the bridge and found something called a Wildlife Management Area (WMA), and pulled in to a small graveled clearing to tinker on the truck.

Normally at this point I would get frustrated with making a simple factual entry, complaining that I'm not sharing anything important, but this is *my* adventure and it's amazing how important all these things seem. I wasted my last weekend in Memphis doing absolutely nothing. Now I'm not even 48 hours into my trip and have already experienced so much I can't even share it all. I know it's cliché but this must be what they mean by "life is in the details." Let's just say that so far I'm not the least bit disappointed with the trip.

I've noticed a few examples of trying too hard. I have to repeat to myself, "Patience Luke" (in the voice of Alec Guinness.) Just then I was juggling "experiencing the details" versus "feeling the buoyancy of shedding stress." My pragmatic side wants to catalog each experience but my spiritual side just wants to experience them. Maybe this will work itself out soon enough. Hopefully with that will come the balance between feeling the need to write something worthwhile and just letting the pen move.

The world is so beautiful this morning. The sky is a perfect gray. At first glance everything seems muted by a light morning fog, until you notice the contrast accentuated by last night's rain. You expect it to be cold but it must be in the 60's. I've spent the last 20-30 minutes enjoying an incredible country breakfast and listening to a table full of good ol' boys bantering clichés of the sort you'd expect they banter every morning. I haven't heard a trolley or a street sweeper or been bombarded by a lifetime of memories for nearly two days. I can only imagine how beautiful the world will become as I shed even more of that. This is why I wanted to spend a few days alone on the road before seeing KB. Towards the end, the stress of simply leaving had added greatly to the stresses I was trying to leave.

Sorry, I completely lost track of relating my adventure. Hopefully I'll get back to that, but right now I'm itching to get back on the road. In case I get sidetracked again, I want to thank the man who stopped to make sure I was okay at the WMA and for offering the fish he had just caught. I'm not sure if it were lingering mistrust or being overwhelmed by such a simple act of kindness, but I almost immediately regretted not accepting it.

*same day 8:50 AM*

I've made it to Quarry Pavilion overlooking Norfolk Lake. When the government finishes selling out to China, I'm coming here to live in the woods, by god. I've found an incredible place to spend the day, lighten the load, bleed the brakes, and grease and tighten anything else I can find. (The Ozarks are no place for spongy brakes and a loose suspension.) I feel like I'm literally on top of the world. The sky is still gray but I'm surrounded by tree covered mountains, sitting under a pavilion with lights and electricity. I have the radio tuned to a local country station for company and am seriously considering spending the day and night. I've also brought out the journal to jot down thought fragments as I go along.

☙

Monday night I made the round of goodbyes to my family, which went much better than expected. My mother's mother just wanted to talk and talk. She made us dinner of leftovers and sliced tomatoes, more delicious than filet mignon. I told her it was very likely she'd be gone before I returned (she's 97) and that I'd probably miss her funeral too. She said she understood. I also told her she was my Yoda and one of the few truly positive influences in my life. I hope when she passes part of her spirit comes to me. She's an utterly sweet, moral woman who any person breathing would love to have for a grandmother.

Then I went next door to see my mother. I asked her if I was abused as a child. She said no, but then again she claimed to not remember beating my brothers and sister, so I don't put a lot of weight on her response. I suppose she's attempting to gain sanity by forgetting the insanity, which is entirely possible, though not entirely stable or healthy. I tried to share part of my "your own well-being is your primary concern" philosophy, but couldn't tell if any of it made it through. She asked several times if I harbored any ill feelings for her. I tried to explain (as civilly as I could) that I basically had *no* feelings for her, that I'm just trying to move on with my life and get away from my family and the readily available barrage of failure excuses. As I was leaving she handed me a small bag of boxed raisins. The gesture of wanting to contribute anything she could to my adventure was touching.

That night I stayed at my dad's. In the morning I asked him to forgive me for leaving just when AO's death and funeral were imminent. I told him I felt pulled towards doing something worthwhile with my life and that my seemingly Bohemian lifestyle had little to do with sex, drugs, and rock-and-roll. I said I could see two potential futures for humanity, both of which will be determined by our actions of today and irrevocably set over the next 20 years, and that I could no longer ignore the feeling I should be doing more to help determine the course. Then my oldest brother (JR) called and asked me to hang around until he got there, but I knew I would bolt as soon as I could.

I never got to see DAB (my "drunk alcoholic brother", as opposed to "recovering alcoholic brother"), although my dad said he's drinking a lot less and has held a steady job for almost a year. Lord knows he's too young to drink himself to death. I told my mother that if she really wanted healing, she should start by apologizing for abusing him as a child, which was the impetus for the self-loathing he is now trying to drown with alcohol. I hope someday humanity realizes the importance of properly fostering our young. Is there any other species that treats their offspring so badly?

*same day 2:08 PM*

I love being in love and at the moment I feel in love with everything. I'm in love with a woman I can't be with and with whom I had no business falling in love in the first place. (For the purpose of this book, let's call her Saint Jane, or SJ.) It is this love that makes me feel comfortable with being alone for the first time in my life. An ex once told me all I've ever done is go from one girlfriend or wife to another, which may have been true at the time I guess. But now I not only know what it's like to be in love, but to be so much in love that it's okay we're not together, or I that have anyone for that matter.

*later that evening*

Sitting here in the back of my truck, surrounded by all my worldly possessions (mostly food, clothes, and art supplies), with the homemade bed cover propped up to form a lean-to shed, I feel more at home than I've ever felt anywhere in my life.

*Monday November 6th 2000*
*Springfield*

The last 2-1/2 days have been fairly uneventful. KB and I didn't do much except go out both Friday and Saturday nights and hang out the rest of the time. We did have a few great conversations, sharing our ideas and visions for the future. I'm now at the Mud House coffee bar in downtown Springfield. They have a $2.00 "bottomless cup", which affords me great opportunity to sit comfortably warm and dry with endless hot java and clean porcelain. One amazing aspect of contemporary civilization is that I can so easily avoid spending this rainy evening in the cab of my pickup, condemned to little more than napping or making a journal entry. Plus the atmosphere here is exquisite.

I suppose it would be good, in terms of making this attempt even halfway substantial, to get on with what I've come to see as the purpose of this trip and journal. First of all the title, *In Search of a New Millennium*, is intended quite literally. For as long as I can remember, the phrase "21st century" has conjured images of a Jetsonian future. But now that we are here nothing seems all that different. So the purpose of my journey is threefold: A. To witness first hand, and hopefully partake in, as many different lifestyles as possible, in as varied an array of locales as possible. There are an untold number of ways of thinking and doing, yet we all tend to get stuck in our own particular way, especially if our world is restricted to one type of people or one part of the country. B. To discover within myself the fundamental elements of what it means to be a self-sufficient, cognitive, spiritually in-tune human being, without the baggage of past suppressions, failures, and fears. and C. To combine these, along with some serious introspection and creative visualization, in an attempt to better understand my role in assisting humanity to avoid what I see as potentially devastating pitfalls in our very near future.

I am what I refer to as a staunch Individualist and a staunch Evolutionist. By Individualist I mean I believe every single person is responsible for ensuring their own well-being and sense of inner peace, happiness, and purpose. Evolutionist means I believe every single event that has ever occurred in the entire history of the cosmos has brought us to this precise moment in time and particular set of circumstances. Evolution drives everything: A species, an ecosystem, the very Earth itself, as well as the individual human being. The only possibility of explaining why this is so, or why it is at all, is to continue experiencing, contemplating, and sharing, in the hope we can discover the answers together, and in the process hopefully inspire one another to follow the right course.

I just spent my last two paper dollars on a huge iced brownie for supper. I'm pretty sure I have enough change in the truck for tomorrow's bottomless cup, but am fairly clueless after that. Although I have a few prospects for work, and a room by the week whenever I can scrape up $135, for now I'm creeping too close to being hungry and homeless. But I'm really enjoying the energy of this place. The energy in Springfield is infinitely more positive than you-know-where, and the basking is good for my soul. I'm sure it will keep you from having to endure as much of the bitching and moaning as before.

## Tuesday November 7th Y2K
### Election day

I am once again wrapped in the arms of paradise, otherwise known as the Mud House, having spent last night in the frigid hell of the cab of my truck. My toes feel like they must have gotten close to frozen, because now they have that painful tingling sensation of thawing.

Last night here was heavenly. About 9:30 or so, I met three local college guys and we talked forever about philosophy and religion. The place was packed too. Tonight I'll try to stay closer to midnight, if only to shorten my frozen torture. I have two potential opportunities for finding work today. I don't mind eating cold canned soup (from storage in the truck), but I'd be lost if I couldn't afford my bottomless cup.

It's occurred to me I should take care not to let my ego sneak too deeply into this experiment. I believe we all have to be our own best friend and biggest fan, the harm comes when this is attempted in a false manner or to the detriment of others.

My god, I swear this place must be taunting me to write. Just as that last paragraph was coming out, in walked an enticingly beautiful woman. She's blonde and thin and apparently of good social skill, but upon closer examination seems plagued by low self-esteem. She's tried to plaster this over with the various accouterments misconstrued by society to convey confidence and beauty, but, as with all things, reality has prevailed.

The single most devastating tendency of man is our attempt to exist outside the bounds of reality. Reality is not an ugly thing, in fact quite the opposite. It's the supposedly inexplicable backlash of reality against our attempts to ignore it that we label as proof of reality's ugliness. Many Western religions have bastardized this to somehow mean life is intended for suffering and that our reward is to come in the afterlife. I say let the dead contemplate death and the living contemplate life.

I'm not sure how deep into a religious discussion I want to get at the moment. It's easier on both of us if I toss out one idea at a time and let it bounce around by itself for a while, instead of trying to get it all out at once - which would only serve to confuse and bore us both. Part of my stifled upbringing makes it difficult to approach anything new without apprehension, which I also see as a prevalent flaw in society, so we'll just take this one step at a time.

For now, ponder the notion that in order for us to reach the more cohesive social awareness required for our mutual survival, the first step is to question everything about our current beliefs and practices. You will not burn in hell for questioning your belief in God or for analyzing the many so-called truths you've been taught. But what greater hell than to wallow day after day in a quagmire of uncertainty, afraid not only to ask, but to know either way. Step out of the swamp and join me on dry land for a while.

I find the more ugliness I purge on the inside, the more ugliness I shed on the outside. This is the one secret no marketing company will ever share, that the beauty and confidence they attempt to portray with air-brushed models and glitzy advertising, can only come from the inside. Not only are their products a laughingly poor substitute, but in fact only serve to perpetuate the evils of mediocrity, for as long as you try to work from the outside in, instead of from the inside out.

Let me stop here and offer two points that may shed some light on what I'm trying to say. First of all, I'm not claiming immunity from the trappings of false beauty, even while understanding that it only serves to postpone our salvation and hasten our decline.

Also, when I use words like "evil" and "salvation", I'm not trying to sound like a Bible thumping, stump preacher. I do not support the concept of evil as a phenomenon unto itself. There is only good and the absence of good. And salvation is not something bestowed upon us from without, but earned by us from within. Salvation is the opposite of destruction, that great unknown we will accomplish once we get ourselves back on the right path. Nothing I speak of is meant to sound distant or impossible, to be accomplished only by faith, but very real and tangible, to be accomplished by reason and determination.

We each face the decision of living in heaven (a truly blissful state) or hell (a deeply fearsome state) every moment of every day. There is no need to postpone the choice until the grave. Now is when we are alive. And now is the only time over which we have even a modicum of control. Our destiny is not in the hands of some celestial puppet master but firmly within our own grasp. Is there a God? I have no idea. But I know if there were, God would not welcome the frail creatures we have become.

*same day 9:30 PM*

In September of '99, I let an out-of-town artist crash at my place while she was in Memphis for an arts festival. It's strange how unfolding events more than a year later have brought us back together. I lost her name and number a long time ago, but today only had to give a partial description of her at the local Arts Council office and they knew exactly who I was talking about. So we met and she offered to let me crash at one of her buildings, an old hotel built in 1907. There's no heat but it beats the hell out of sleeping in the truck.

Right now I'm watching the presidential election results at the local IBEW. It's interesting to be in such a locally prominent place for this, although deep down I don't support either Gore or Bush. They're both just groomed puppets trained for little more than pandering and compromise.

*Wednesday November 8th Y2K 10:08 PM,
Cotton's on Commercial*

Things are going great! Today I landed a consulting gig with a local engineer acquaintance *and* got a cash advance!

I wish I felt like bringing you up to speed or spouting a little BS, but at the moment I really don't. I'm more in the mood of just absorbing the atmosphere of my new neighborhood bar. It's felt incredible to be free of the old ghosts. Now I'm just trying to be content, or at least discover what the word even means. I've committed to staying in Springfield six more weeks, but that should be okay. I can save some money, get the truck even more road ready, and continue to wash the stench of you-know-where off me.

૭૩

I love you. I catch myself saying it a lot. Part of me would give anything to be with you. But this is my adventure and I have to do it alone. I only wish I had some way of telling you how much you are with me, some way of asking if you still think of me. In my mind you do, but my love is for you, not for what you may still feel for me. If you are happy, that's all that matters. I once told you I had nothing to offer my Ideal and it's true more so now than ever. Part of why I am seeking this better version of myself is so if I ever get the chance to say, "I give you all that I am", I'll be offering something of value.

*Next night, new bar, Ruthie's.
Only Busch on tap and karaoke!*

Even though I'm on this quest to find my better self, and even if by chance some of the things that spill onto the page turn out to be worth a damn, in the end I'm just a man. If there is a difference, it's that I believe there is a miraculously beautiful, creative, intelligent, and passionate being at the core of each of us, and anything less in our adult selves is the result of improper childhood or social influences. And I believe life is an incredible gift, meant to be *lived*, not simply endured.

I also believe deep down on the inside we all know this to be true. That these principles are the essence of what it means to be human. Why we continue to struggle feeling anything less is beyond me.

*Monday November 13th 2000 5:50 PM*

Do I use my grandiose visions of mankind and the future simply to mask something lacking in myself? Of course I then have to ask what difference does it make? I realize my notions of man are idealistic, but my god, we have to strive for something. We need to have some idea of where we want to go. We have to be able to see beyond our immediate horizon if we're ever going to avoid running in circles.

I guess I'm just depressed, which always makes me hard on myself. What's worse is I can rarely define why I'm depressed. And it's not a debilitating feeling, just a lower level of "normal" than normal. Sometimes it's my bad habit baggage dragging me down. I need time to adjust to this whole adventure thing and learn to work with the various realities as they come along. I spend a great deal of time in fantasy mode, which is good for developing visions but bad for accepting day to day realities.

I've been trying to consider emotion's role in our future. I know we will be less fragile than we are now, and less fragile means less needy. As such, our emotional interactions will be more intimate and supportive. But I need these things now. I can manage waiting for more ideal living conditions, but longing for more ideal emotional interaction is harder to handle. Maybe the path to our idealistic future begins with emotional intimacy on a social scale?

*Wednesday November 15th 7:00 AM,
Hamby's Steakhouse*

Well, the adventure continues. Last night was miserable. I've rented space in an old firehouse, but again there is *no heat*! Last night I froze my butt off until I decided to sleep in the landlady's office upstairs, which is the only heated space. But god bless early morning diners, although I can't highly recommend this one.

I need to decide how long to continue this exercise. I've already thought about most of what I want to share, my ideas of future society and what it will take to get us there. So what's left? Can I honestly assume you will have any interest in my petty little adventure? Can I anticipate experiencing anything of note?

What I most hope to accomplish is to see life beyond the trivial necessities of being settled, beyond romance, and beyond dealing with my family. In the process I hope to develop a deeper, more honest assessment of myself, simultaneously combining the positive elements of the "real me" with my idealistic visions of the "ultimate me", as part of what I see as a pragmatic process of developing the best me that I can.

Then there's the hope of exhilarations like sun rises, skinny dipping, engrossed conversations, and seeing the Grand Canyon. So regardless of what may or may not come of this journey, I'll keep you with me until I finally make it to the Grand Canyon. I've long since felt something calling me there, some spirit fluttering around leaving images inside my head. But let's not get overly enthusiastic, I don't want to feel let down when I'm finally there. Maybe that's another theme I should work on. I spend so much time dreaming about how wonderful life *can* be, that much of what's left is wasted being disappointed with life as it is.

*same day 10:30 PM*

Sorry I haven't cut loose in a few days. I know my best work comes when the pen just moves across the page and I'm completely lost in watching the ink flow. Maybe it's difficult for me to be completely honest right now. Or maybe I'm feeling things I don't want to share. Hard to say.

*Saturday November 18th,
Year of Our Lord 2000 AD*

Of all the cool things I've done in my life, this ranks right up there with the coolest. I have the truck pulled halfway into one of the big bay doors of the firehouse with the Springfield Christmas parade coming at me from the left and turning at the T-intersection right in front of me. I'm sitting on the homemade bed cover watching the parade from my own private little perch. Here comes a marching band! It just doesn't get any better than this.

Evidently someone decided it's not good to toss candy directly at the spectators, so they just sort of splay it on the ground and the kids dive for it. What fun!

A team of Clydesdales pulling a red wagon just did a 360 in the intersection right in front of me!

Elvis just rode by on a float!

Someone put a porta-potty on the back of a trailer and covered it with Christmas decorations to make it look like a small house. Some poor kid is sticking his head out the door and waving to the crowd. I swear I'm in heaven!

Twelve, count 'em, twelve identical, fully restored '65 Mustang convertibles just went by in a pack!

Pride. Fierce, unflinching pride. Pride is what makes the flag girl hold her head high and the percussionist beat the hell out of his drum, and is the only thing that has ever served to lift us out of the naïve bliss of the animal world.

One hour and seven minutes later and it's all over. It was grand while it lasted!

*Sunday November 19th 2000*

I've been pretty mellow all day. It's feels like I'm watching a movie of my life and only cautiously participating from the sidelines as events unfold. Like moving in a fog but the fog is an enveloping mist of fate, and the slightest movement off key would irrevocably alter everything. Like I've entered a room that's dominated by one of those ripple action special effects.

I would have in fact slept all day had my landlady not come by. I was lying on my borrowed inflatable mattress, daydreaming about being on the road asking some diner manager if I could do an odd job for a meal, when at that very moment she came in and asked if I could help fix a water heater.

I had a revelation the other day. Literally. I was walking down the street and, as I turned my head to glance behind me, a flash of reflected sunlight hit me right in the eyes and immediately seared this thought onto my brain: There are so many options and so many ways to improve and so many things to experience and so many ways to contribute to the evolution of my species, that it's impossible to quantify what an "ultimate" me would even look like.

*Tuesday November 21st 8:45 PM,*
*Mud House*

Last night I met a young woman who's a student at a local Bible college. We had a great chat about religion, at the end of which, I swear to god, she tried to witness to me! Oh poor misguided child. I tried to explain that I've already been in her shoes and have simply grown to see beyond the rhetoric and dogma.

If we are ever to reach the new millennium, we must first evolve a more intelligent (not rooted in on caveman superstitions), spiritual (not driven by moral or social weaknesses), balanced (regain the Divine Feminine), and cohesive (meld the Eastern and Western), religion. Organized religions have been misused for political and divisive means far too long.

One of the catch 22's of many religions is first they tell you to ignore the temptation of questioning what you're taught, then they say if you don't believe on blind faith you'll burn in hell. And the clincher is that matters of faith - like the very existence of God - cannot be understood by mere mortal man. So with their inquisitive nature crippled from birth, practitioners are left to flounder through life, never understanding yet never questioning, and labeling their inevitable failures as innate human weakness.

CB

Perhaps the most important concept in defining the new millennial society, one that gets more difficult to grasp as the global population continues to grow, is the importance of every single individual life. Beware the tendency to take life, any life, for granted, for to wait until the moment of death before you truly understand what it means to be alive, is to render moot every moment to that point.

*Wednesday 8:00 PM,*
*Lilly's Steakhouse in Ava, Missouri*

Hobbling my way to Jonesboro to meet up with my nephew (let's call him OB) and sister-in-law to go back to Memphis for a combination Thanksgiving dinner and wake for AO tomorrow night. My father called today and, by his tone, I felt compelled to go. The least I can hope for is to run the truck off the road, although if this actually happens, it was an accident! (In this part of the country you can be 100 feet closer to hell faster than you can piss your pants - my impression of what it's like to drive an old pickup through Ozark Mountain back roads.) I'm just not ready to deal with my family, but at least they'll all be together and maybe I can pull off a final "so long, kiss my ass" in one fell swoop.

But I'm sure it won't be that bad. I anticipate decent conversation with my sister and nephew and maybe even DAB. I'll stop by and see my grandmother one more time. I'm just thankful AO's suffering is finally over. She was a woman with nothing if not dignity and did not deserve to waste away as she did.

*Sunday November 26th 5:30 PM,*
*back at Mud House*

My little adventure within an adventure was pretty strange. I left Springfield Wednesday night and took back roads to just the good side of Hardy, Arkansas, where I found the coolest Mom-n-Pop motel for only $25. After I made it to JR's in Jonesboro Thursday morning, we all piled into their family minivan and drove to my dad's for Thanksgiving dinner. The entire extended family was there, but luckily everyone was focused on AO and didn't give me any grief.

Friday was a day full of Looney Tunes back at JR's, then visitation at the funeral home (in Jonesboro) that afternoon.

Then my dad woke me up at 3:45 in the morning to say he was going *back* to Memphis to get a different suit. (I later found out the trip was to "visit" my mother, but I won't get into that.)

This is only relevant because we had to meet JR later that morning to dig AO's grave! Can you believe it?! Before, I had only been to funerals where the tent, chairs, and Astroturf, were all already in place. You didn't even notice there was a hole beneath the casket, much less try to deal with the fact you were just standing *in* the goddamned thing! If you've never dug a grave (and no one I've spoken to has), one gruesome part of the job is getting down inside to measure the bottom. There are few experiences creepier than standing in a 3' x 8' x 6' hole that before the sun sets will inter your stepmother's corpse for all eternity.

Then on the drive back to Springfield earlier today, in a diner in Viola, Arkansas, I saw myself 40 years into the future. This cool looking old man (boots, overalls, jean jacket, and cap, we'll call him 77) pulled up in an old Ford Model A (roughly 40 years younger than my truck), walked in without saying a word, picked up a to-go order, and walked out. I do occasionally feel enough contempt for society to want to spend the next 40 years just keeping to myself, but this is impossible for two reasons:  A. I believe I understand the root cause of many of man's troubles, and as such, also believe I know the cure. and   B. I don't see society remaining intact without changing our present course. And what right would I have to complain if I felt these things and did nothing?

*Monday November 27th 9:00 PM,*
*Mud House*

There's this louder, older wannabe who is hogging the bulk of the conversation at the table right behind me. Although I can't see him, I bet he's thin, with short, curly, reddish-brown hair and cropped beard, glasses, plaid shirt, and light brown eyes.

He has one of those voices that pierces through all other sounds around it as surely as it pierces the air. Unfortunately, it's also impossible to completely ignore. He seems to require validation from his younger comrades and is engaging in the conversational equivalent of dangling a ball of string over a cat. Lots of activity on the surface, but no real interaction or interest.

Well, except for not looking that much older than his friends, and the shirt being a brown casual pullover, everything else was dead on, right down to the fact I knew he would look up as I passed (hence the reference to eye color.) People are so painfully predictable. That's why I'm fascinated by the rare complex people I meet. Of course people are *capable* of infinite depth, most simply choose the easy road, or what they think is the easy road.

*Tuesday November 28th 6:00 PM*

I'm meeting tonight with a lady who has a place in the country and is looking for "earthy intellectual" roommates. Earlier I had visions of running naked through the snow and belly flopping into a pond about 100 yards or so out the back door down a sloping hill. So on the phone today I said, "And if you have a pond about 100 yards or so out the back door down a sloping hill, I'm really going to freak", and she DID! I'm telling you man, this vision thing is incredible!

03

I've had a good evening at the ole' Mud House. One of the philosophy guys from a few chapters back dropped in, although he seemed too high-strung tonight for in-depth conversation. But the lady with the house never showed. I'm not sure what's up with that. Oh well, it's time to scoot anyway. Goodnight!

## Thursday November 30th

At Outland across the street from the Mud House, waiting for what sounds like a damned fine blues-funk-jazz trio to start. I want to share a few random thoughts that've been wafting around inside my skull as I've been otherwise engaged in traveling to funerals and earning a living...

Rules: Living your life by all the rules established by society but never questioning them, and then wondering why things continue to go wrong and why you are so dissatisfied with life. I recently had a work related meeting with a woman who was a perfect case study of this. She had a droopy, sullen look about her. The flesh of her face was like bacon that had been left out on the counter too long, all limp and slimy. Watching her in the meeting was like trying to watch a swimmer in a pool of molasses. Not only was there no "pep in her step", but every movement seemed a struggle. Even though I can often rightly be accused of over dramatizing, this is a fairly accurate description.

After the meeting, we were making small talk and she told me her husband had recently gotten fired after such-n-such many years on the job. I specifically remember her using the phrase, "We followed all the rules, only to get shafted in the end." So now, instead of enjoying the romanticized retirement they had put off for so long, they both have to keep working.

I realize part of the problem here lies with the employer who gave them the shaft, but a larger part lies with them. See, the bacon look didn't come from this one incident, but from years of attempting to squelch her inner passions in favor of following someone else's rules, of striving for some long-off goal at the expense of her immediate desires. I'm not sure how often I've said this so far, or if I even have, but I will say it here regardless: No one outside of your skin can have any bearing whatsoever on your existence that you do not specifically grant them. You, and you alone, are responsible for your own happiness and well-being.

Now this exorbitant freedom may not apply if you were unfortunate enough to have been born in China or some third world dictatorship, but if you're reading this, then chances are you weren't. *So why are you squandering your God-given freedom on being a mindless, soulless, passionless, human bovine?!*

Diversity: We've all heard the talk about self-mimicking society and, "You don't want everyone to be the same, do you?", but what about the flipside of this? What if there were no wife beaters or rapist or child pornographers? Would that be so bad? Do we really need diversity that badly? Think about it. True diversity stems from the acceptance of others, regardless of where their inner passions may lead them. Unfortunately, many misinterpret this to also include actions used to mask inner pain. As a society, we need to take care not to overemphasize acceptance to the point of failing to heed the pain.

What's next?: I will admit that at this point it's difficult for me to visualize humanity's advancement once we've evolved to the point of making MegaCities not only possible, but thriving. I can see us reveling in creativity, self-discovery, brilliance, radiance, affection, and intimacy, but what will come from this? And that's the beauty of it. MegaCity is only the first step, our toe-hold on the spring board of the next phase of human evolution.

Evolution: Evolution is happening, has always happened, and will always happen. There is a Life force driving evolution, most evident in the inconceivable complexity of the web of life as it has come to exist. Although man is merely one small part of this web, we are the only living creatures with the capacity to manipulate evolution, to not only envision our future but to make it happen. Do you even have a clue what this means? It means that for as long as we continue to accept the weaknesses and flaws we fabricated and have tolerated for the last 5,000 years, they will continue to hold us back. But the very second we refuse to accept them, they will vanish!

I have an experiment for you. Take a minute and reach back to that beautiful child you were at birth. Try to grasp the awesome wonder with which you faced life at the time. Go back to before you realized your parents weren't perfect, before you were spoon fed what they wanted you to believe, before anyone convinced you of the futility of individual effort or the pursuit of real, unabashed joy. Before you learned of mankind's long history of self-loathing and self-defeat. Back when you could spend hours playing with a grasshopper, when the sun on your face was ample excuse for laughing and dancing. *Be* that child again for one split second and you will Know. Life is meant to be wonderful! Everything we've been led to believe to the contrary was wholly concocted and perpetuated by those who were dissatisfied with their own existence, and thus set out to dupe others into feeling as miserable as themselves.

Ever since the first disgruntled, unprepared parent beat or under-appreciated or ignored or under-loved or under-stimulated their child, those children have grown to be underdeveloped (or just plain twisted) human'esque creatures. And as such, have created phenomena adopted by subsequent generations intended for no other purpose but to cripple the development of otherwise joyous, more fulfilled and fully developed human beings. The confusion you've wrestled with silently your entire life, is the beautiful divine seed of your True Self refusing to accept the ignorance and insanity you see all around you. You find it impossible to believe the murders, rapes, and babies in dumpsters, and "logically" attribute it to the innate weakness of man. What no one has ever told you is that even this "logic" is a merely concoction of the weak.

Don't believe me? Look around. Nowhere else in the entire animal kingdom will you see examples of what we have come to call evil. There are no murders in nature. Animals kill other animals as an evolved and necessary fragment of the overall web of life. Just because we have evolved the capacity to *choose* to murder, is no reason to believe we have a genetic predisposition to murder. Evolution is a continual progression towards theoretical perfection. Does it look like we are progressing towards theoretical perfection? I don't think so.

I had not intended to get into all that so soon, it just started coming out while sucking caffeine. I still don't feel like I've finished. All I can guess at this point is an even deeper revelation to come. Some backhand to the knees, asphalt in the gash on the back of my skull, revelation. Maybe it's an understanding of what's to come next. Hopefully it's a more concrete idea of the role I am meant to play. Maybe the apocalypse will loom imminent before I can make it to the Grand Canyon, thereby releasing my Chicken Little mode of hedging off as much damage as possible, by sharing the above with as many souls as will listen. After all, there's nothing like a little serious trauma to force one to embrace one's Inner Child and open one's fucking mind.

But this is getting too close to the whammy. I've expended a great deal of energy in the last two hours and now must go. I'm sure you're exhausted too. Maybe you should reread that last part a few times. Try to go off by yourself and squelch the doubting reverberations in your mind. Breathe like a child. Inhale joy. Smile. You will come to understand. You will come to believe. As for me, I'm about to witness three beautiful souls express themselves through music. And it's amazing, but with the last two words of that last sentence, I completely filled the first sketchpad journal. (I'm now scribbling on the inside of the front cover.) If that's not a sure sign of the end of phase one of my adventure, I don't know what is. With any luck, you're at least partly as excited as I am to see what's to come. In the meantime, relax. Hug your kids, kiss your wife, quit your job.

In other words get a life, create a life, *live* a life. Smile, dance, laugh, and sing. But above all, praise, nurture, and love a child. They are our only hope.

# Book II

*Friday December 1st 2000*

Welcome to Book II, which just means I've started a new sketchpad journal. The band last night was incredible *and* I danced my fanny off! This was the kind of place where everybody's in front of the stage dancing and nobody gives a damn. You should definitely try it sometime. Peel back your inhibitions, dance and feel the rhythm of your soul. No matter your what accepted lot in life, you will enjoy it.

And sad news sports fans. I just glanced at a leftover fragment of today's sports page and saw Tampa Bay is favored by ten over Dallas this weekend. If that's not a sure sign of the apocalypse, I don't know what is. When I was a kid the Cowboys were the undisputed gods of football and Tampa Bay was the league joke.

You know what I'd like to do? I want to find the lowest ranked team in the NFL and step in as head coach for one season. I would never punt on 4th down unless inside my own 20. I would inspire the team to play each down as if it were the last play of the Super Bowl and we were behind by 6 on the 3rd yard line. Any fan can appreciate the mental stamina required to give 115%, play after play, smack dab in the middle of a losing season.

Psst… Want to know the secret? It's all in the mind. And *that* is the pertinent issue. It's always all in the mind. Your job, how you perceive your marital situation, your own sense of self-worth, the gusto with which you seize the day, all of it. If your mind's not right, nothing is right. Get your mind straight and the rest will follow. Determine to prevail and you will win, accept defeat and you will lose. Was there anything less in Bear Bryant's philosophy? Can you imagine how far our country would go if we had a Bear Bryant as President? But no, we have two pansies to choose from (and as I write, they're still spatting it out like two third graders at recess.) How can the United States of America maintain our role as global leader with spineless jellyfish like Gore or Bush at the helm?

### *Thursday December 7th 2000*

A little voice is gnawing at me that I'm avoiding something. I know somewhere between the current me and the ultimate me, lies a hurdle of serious self-doubt. I don't broach the subject often, but I know it's there. Like the deepest root of my negative programing that can only be remedied by digging deep enough to get out all of it. Some long buried trait that knows it's easier to envision something than to do it, resulting in an endless cycle of delusion and procrastination. Neither of these are healthy or have anything to do with this more better me I am seeking.

Remember the fog episode from a Sunday or two ago? I'm feeling it again. In the past, my tendency has been to run full steam with whatever notion the fog was revealing, which, more often than not, ended up with me eating asphalt. Although all of my sequential crashes eventually got me to where I am now, I can't say I thoroughly enjoyed it. As such, I have become leery of running with anything. The purpose of this adventure is to allow myself, as much as possible, to follow my own nose. But I also have a convenient escape clause. For the time being at least, I neither need nor want to get involved in anything that requires substantial commitment.

଼ଷ

If I thought I were free to, I could let fly with some real cheese...

My mind, my heart, and my soul, are each deep dark pools of cool water, like filled wells. I am totally engulfed in the water. All is peaceful and dark around me. Nothing on the outside matters or even exists. I am completely within myself and in tune. When I am engaged in a challenging project, I swim in the mind pool. I'm bombarded by concepts and insights that have nothing to do with the project that provided the initial stimulus. When I am in love, I swim in the heart pool. There is nothing I wouldn't do for the woman I love. My devotion is complete, and as a result I feel my life is more complete. When I drive my truck over a hill into the setting sun, my soul reaches up and envelopes *me*. Swimming in this sense is an understatement, it's more akin to the very caress of God. On a few rare occasions I have experienced all three in unison. Everything is beautiful. I feel like I'm glowing, moving in slow motion and watching myself from on high at the same time. I am invincible, because all concept of harm or death or anything remotely contrary to joy is nonexistent.

If I could put into words what I see as the ultimate me, it would be to feel this way all the time. I know I have it in me. I know we all do, for we are born with it. It is only doubt and fear that keeps us from it. We flounder around half alive, thinking of life as some cruel joke, more wrapped up in our own self-pity than the beauty that's all around us.

The God so many have sought externally for eons, lives in part in all of us. All we need do is open our own inner vault and release. Forget that you feel threatened by those who display little weakness and realize you have the capacity for strength yourself. Stop envying those who enjoy their natural intelligence and start enjoying your own. Stop repeating the zombie mantras and start listening to the wind rustling through the trees. Stop worrying about what brand of clothes are on your back and start getting some sun on your face. And sing goddamnit! If you could only feel one small fragment of the vibrant energy of Life, I know you would be as crazed for it as I am.

And remember, I know your secret. You think no one Knows and everyone around you is riddled with doubt and fear, and thus consider it our "natural" state, while at the same time not quite believing anyone could be as fragile as yourself. But once or twice in your life, early in the morning all cozy in bed, you have longed for peace. You have wondered what joy would feel like. But then you got up, started your daily routine, and immediately slipped back into your melancholic state of mind. You recognize a paraplegic as being physically handicapped, but fail to see that by merely existing in your zombie state you are spiritually (and as a result, morally) handicapped. But unlike the paraplegic who longs to climb mountains, you freely ignore any possibility of joy.

I have said too much. You already know everything I've tried to say anyway, it's not up to me to explain it. You are human, you are inside your skin. You are the only one living your life, and you are the only one capable of altering it. I could say the words that reveal the meaning of life, but until *you* hear the words and until *you* absorb them and take them to heart, any effort on my part is pointless. My adventure is completely for my own benefit. I am listening and absorbing and utilizing my own life lessons. I can attempt to share, I can feel some responsibility to my fellow humans, or I could delude the hell out of myself and bore the hell out of you. Either way the same is true. I am living my life, you are living yours. We can make this experience more enjoyable for one another, or more difficult. We are an evolved bipedal species living as part of a magnificently complex organism called Earth. We got here somehow, we are going somewhere. But for now, all of our conscious awareness is engaged in experiencing this phenomenon we call life. We don't know all the reasons why. We have created religions in homage to some of our theories. We have created sciences to study what we think we can. But all the while, we live. And for as long as we are alive, I contend it is within our grasp to do so joyously. The misery you see as so concrete is an illusion. We created suffering, we can rid ourselves of it.

Let me put it this way: Every single aspect of life and our experiences of it, can be as beautiful as cool jazz. It is not just a brief flicker in an otherwise dank fog, but a tangible example of the way things should be. Embrace it. Embrace it with me. The love that is waiting for you will obliterate the meaninglessness and the pain.

*Wednesday December 13th 7:50 AM*

There is 8" of snow on the ground in Springfield and I'm snowbound at the firehouse. How is man supposed to live in these conditions? I'd rather be laying on the beach in South Padre¹, which is where I'm headed after I visit my daughter (CL) in Orlando for Christmas. I have a giddiness bubbling its way up, which I consider a sign I'm doing something right. I love feeling giddy, even if it is partly due to the snow.

I seem to have been given a day for writing, but all I really want to do is hole-up in front of a TV with a huge bowl of Cracker Jacks and warm rum and Dr. Pepper. It's odd how we tend to miss opportunities that present themselves, simply because we're stuck on engrained patterns. How do you juggle between following the signs and making your own way? For instance, it was a good example of following the signs that led me to King Biscuit and to KB and eventually to Springfield, but it is more an example of making my own way that has made my stay here so enjoyable.

☙

Last night I had an incredible conversation with a young revolutionary who wants to organize anti-corruption protests in Washington. I shared with him my "X" theory, which is a diagrammatic representation of time and events. The top half of the "X" represents everything that has ever happened, the bottom half represents everything that *will* ever happen. The point of intersection represents this precise moment in time. It is meant to illustrate the fact that everything that has ever happened throughout history, has brought us to this precise moment and set of circumstances that we know as our individual lives and the human world around us. And our actions of this moment have a direct impact on everything that will ever happen from this point on.

The primary flaw I see with contemporary society is that far too many fail to realize the impact of their actions, or inactions, on the overall course of human evolution. By disregarding entire swatches of life (commonly referred to as wasting time) or spending 1/4 of our lives at jobs we can't stand, only to seek any form of entertainment as a pitiful justification (the "working for the weekend" mentality), we completely disregard our individual responsibility to humanity. When employment and entertainment define our every action, personal growth is removed from the equation. Without personal growth there is no positive dynamic. Without the positive dynamic (the exercised choice to evolve), there is at best a stagnation and at worst a regression, which, if left unchecked, can only lead to our eventual downfall.

And the "whammy" I eluded to before is precisely that. I see the next 20 years of our shared existence as being crucial to the next 200. We are at a point in our social, technological, economic, religious, and political evolutions, where every single movement sends instant reverberations around the globe. The advent of technology, the globalization of economies, and exponential population growth, combine to make our times extremely volatile. Every move we make has a profound impact on everything around us, even if we sit on our asses and do nothing.

The world is changing at lightning speed. Every day we see new developments that foreshadow the world to come. You hear many talk of nuclear annihilation, the mushrooming of Internet porn, massive starvation in third world countries, political and corporate corruption, inner-city gang warfare, insane human rights violations in China and Tibet, and Tampa Bay favored by 10 over the Cowboys. But can you not see where all this is taking us? Can you not see that by continuing down our present path we are certain to face even harsher times, right up to the point of our mutual destruction? Can you see any alternative?

Can you not also see that by merely going through your daily routine, thereby failing to do your part to put humanity back on the right path, that you are by default contributing to your own demise? And if you take all the people who share this rut (and I put the number somewhere between 50-80%), then you begin to see the impact this aggregate meaninglessness has on the course of human evolution. Because for every person who fails to contribute to the positive dynamic, there is another who is all too eager to fill the void, usually with some form of pandering or vice. And your failure to contribute negates your right to complain. And I hate to say it, but pulling a 9 to 5 just to don your kids in Tommy Hilfiger is not sufficient excuse. For what are they going to do except grow up and do the same thing? And it will be your grandchildren who face the desolation you failed to prevent. Talk about burning in hell. What greater hell could there possibly be than knowing you brought life to someone *and* aided in their destruction all in the same breath.

It's okay. Close your eyes. Laugh and think of my words as esoteric BS. But don't cry to me when reality comes a calling. And it *will* come. Maybe it will be in the form of your daughter becoming a crack addicted prostitute, or maybe some punk will shoot your wife in a ritual gang initiation. Maybe our façade economy and political structure will collapse and China will assume the throne of global superpower. Who knows? But understand this: For as long as you sit idly by and do nothing, or for as long as your primary focus is on mindless pursuits, you are fueling the very fires that will bring about your own end.

Oh yeah, there's one more thing, mother nature will only let us piss down her back for so long before she chooses to act in her own defense. Think we can destroy the planet and still live here? Think you can profit from environmental ruin and make enough money to buy clean drinking water when it's gone? Sorry.

So there you have it. The whammy. Either we live or we die. And the time has come that we either live or die together. Our lives and destinies are too intertwined to turn back now. Think the rain forest can burn and not affect us? Sorry. Think those pathetic third-world children you see on TV can all starve without impacting your child's life? Nope. Think it doesn't matter that the shirt you just bought for your kid was sewn by an 8 year old slave girl in India or that 80% of the tag price went straight into the pockets of those who would gladly propel us over the cliff rather than give up their façade existence?

Absolutely every action of every single one of us is interrelated and directly affects our mutual future. Think Nikes make you cool? I thought this country has already dealt with slavery. Think pro-athletes are where it's at? Ask yourself why we pay athletes millions to entertain us and pay teachers a comparative pittance to teach us. Answer? We have been conditioned to seek our hero outside of ourselves. We've been taught to cheer the shallow "accomplishments" of others and decry their failures, instead of cheering our own strengths and faithfully rooting out our own weaknesses. I'll be glad when this situation is remedied, and like everything else I harp on, it eventually will be, one way or the other.

But it doesn't have to be this way. We made the choices required to create the world as we know it and we can make the choices required to correct it. We can either continue to storm down the path to obliteration or we can retreat from the abyss and begin to live life as it was meant to be. There is not one among us who does not crave peace, however we may try to disguise it. There is not one among us who would not benefit from a display of honest affection. There is no life that would suffer from an influx of passion and intelligence. We all know this to be true, yet we continue to neglect these basic human needs. And the resultant creatures lacking such fulfillment are the very ones who are overtly hastening our demise.

I know of no other way to put it. If you need a parable or screenplay with underlying meaning, I'm not the proper source. I am in search of a new millennium and the millennium is upon us. Are we ready? Are we prepared to act according to our mutual interest, to bring about a more fulfilling and meaningful future, or are we going to go gentle into that dark night? The choice is yours to make and the choice is mine to make. But remember, it is impossible for your choice not to affect me. And I could be your mother, your son, or your great-great-granddaughter.

Do not let our supposed advanced intelligence trick you into believing we are somehow above the laws of nature. Do not be drunk when the world crumbles around you and pretend you didn't know. Do not slave away your life, putting off until retirement to learn to play guitar, only to die at 70. Do not deceive yourself into giving up a promising musical career to pursue what you see as your station in life. If the fire of your soul dies, humanity dies with you. In the immortal words of Memphis Minnie, "Cryin' won't help you, prayin' won't do you no good." In the end you will reap what you sow. There is no forgiveness for your sins. Your karmic debt will have to be paid. Withhold your fire from humanity and a cold reality will be the result. Give your share and we all benefit. The life we are meant to live has nothing to do with poverty or crime or perceived human frailties or pornography or drugs or self-loathing. These things came to pass with the first person who sought a mundane existence and have snowballed because so many have unwittingly followed suit. But they would vanish if we simply stopped teaching them to our young, as they are not a natural part of human existence.

Now that I've shared just about everything I had foreseen sharing with this effort, I'm not sure what else I have to offer, other than perhaps a few elaborations on a positive future. I'm not comfortable describing a negative future and hopefully have made my point in that regard. The Grand Canyon is still a few months away, as I'm going to wait out the winter swinging a hammer or pulling pints in South Padre'. I have a few other thoughts I might share, but right now I need a nap. Although I've thoroughly enjoyed writing for the past 2 1/2 hours, my brain is now frazzled and longing to drift off into peaceful oblivion.

*later same evening*

Ever feel like you're in a movie and are absolutely certain the next scene is going to be important? Or has life ever seemed so surreal that it simply must be? I've discovered another neighborhood bar that tops all the rest: Frisco. I feel like the only possible explanation is I've stumbled onto a movie set where the screenwriter wanted to display one of every human dreg there is, and I've been thrust into the cast for comic relief. Remember in Rocky Horror, when Brad first stuck his head around the castle door? That's how I felt 15 minutes ago. But as with most things, I've over-dramatized and probably missed something. A few minutes ago I was sure I was about to get a pool cue wrapped around my head for being an outsider, and a candy-ass at that. Now everyone else is going about their business, while I choke down my Sprite and microwaved cheeseburger. It's times like these I feel it might be better to get into a good old fashioned bar fight than only engage in shallow surface interaction.

The guys behind me are talking about how, "If god came here, he could whoop the whole place." What a living hell it must be to believe in that sort of god. No wonder they drink and spend the bulk of their days afraid of their own shadow.

*Thursday*

One bad thing about the MegaCity environment is so much will be virtual (games, entertainment, education, etc.) that "real" experiences will need to be supplemented. That's why maintaining land in public trust will be so important. Although life in a self-contained MegaCity can sound fairly constricting, ventures into nature will still be an important part of life - one currently missing from many urbanite's lives. My problem is I've always put a premium on comfort. Not pure pussy-foot comfort like insisting on real feather pillows and stuff like that, but a steady, basic comfort. The consequence of this is I miss a lot of raw experiences. Obviously this adventure is an attempt to remedy that and to get a little more stank on me.

One of these days I'm going to take a minute to try and alleviate a few of those psychological concerns I know has to have cropped up while you've been reading this. Like for instance why I'm so certain affection is such an essential part of human existence? I'm sure a few armchair psychologists out there have mumbled to themselves something to the effect that people tend to project their subconscious needs on the world around them. And since my life drastically lacks affection, and always has, it's easy to see how I could be guilty of this.

My model for the ideal human is the newborn. We are never again as sensorially and cognitively viable as we are at birth. The newborn knows nothing of race or poverty or ignorance or social castes or frailties. The human newborn only knows Life, in the fullest sense of the word. And since the newborn benefits greatly from affection - and is in fact stymied without it – it's only natural to assume adults would equally benefit.

*Monday December 25th 2000*

It's now Christmas and I'm at CL's in Orlando. This is the first Christmas she and I have woken up in the same house since her mother and I separated, which was between her first Christmas and first birthday. I know it's been almost two weeks since my last entry. It's not that anything of note hasn't happened in that time, it's just that I've had a lot on my mind. If this were the old me and I were in kicking myself mode, I would say I was either procrastinating or losing interest, but the truth is sometimes you just have to let things jell. Obviously I've wrestled with the notion of who am I to attempt such an undertaking as this book? I am no learned scholar, no theologian or philosopher. I'm not even as well-read or as socially exposed as I would like. Needless to say, I realize I am making a gross assumption by thinking I have anything worthy to add to the vast body of human social consciousness.

*Saturday December 30th 2000 3:15 PM*

Everything I have been attempting to relate so far shares three basic laws: A. All things are connected, you and the planet, actions and reactions, good and evil, etc. B. Every single action of every single one of us ripples endlessly throughout the entire course of human evolution. and C. It is our perceptions and fundamental beliefs that need to change.

We are each born with a profound joy of life. In the beginning, there is nothing required outside of ourselves to experience this joy. But we eventually become conditioned to accept a daily routine and fear oriented need for social status, both of which conspire to squelch our inner joy. This to the point that contemporary society has become little more than a hideous circus of the masses rushing to perpetuate this illusion for one another. And we, in our despair, call this civilization. We work at jobs we hate, just to buy junk we don't need. The profits are then pooled by corporate conglomerates to provide the financial power to further promote the myth of shallow success through uninspired material consumption. This practice only serves to misdirect our attention away from the true meaning of life, which, in case you haven't picked up on it by now, is personal growth and development.

For as long as we continue to attempt our façade existence - personal, social, economic, religious, political, and otherwise - we will continue barreling down the path to self-destruction. And until each and every one of us sheds our socially fabricated frailties and refocuses on the sheer joy of life, we stand no chance of reversing these self-immolating tendencies. My solution is simply this:

## S T O P

This deceptively simple representation of a fundamental truth has two meanings. One is quite literally to stop. You say Exxon is poisoning the environment? I say those in charge can overcome their individual frailties, embrace their own inner joy, and as a result, will not only stop, but will spend the rest of their days working to undo their past wrongs. Politicians are corrupt you say? Need I repeat my rebuttal in order for you to get the point? Every human frailty, from drug addiction to white collar crime, is a direct result of a detachment from our innate inner joy of life. This detachment is the end result of generations of social pressures and misperceptions. The magnitude of malevolence is directly proportionate to the degree of detachment. But the seed kernel of joy remains. And for as long as you draw a breath, it is your ultimate reason for doing so. Another secret I'll throw in here is that the level to which you are either in-tune with or detached from your inner joy, not only manifests itself in your physical being, but in the circumstances of your life as well.

The other meaning of S T O P is: Spend Today Observing Peace. Sounds simple doesn't it? I hate to burst the bubbles of all those deep thinkers out there, but yes, it really is that simple.

Think poisoning the planet is a peaceful activity? Nope. Think funneling illegal campaign contributions into political war chests is peaceful? Sorry. But if the individuals responsible for these activities were to spend each day observing peace, the activities would stop. At this point you say, "Sure, but then someone else would simply take their place." Which is why I stress that the actions of *every* individual impacts humanity, both the actions of those currently responsible and of those who would take their place, as well as the *inaction* of the masses who simply accept the status quo. But the healing has to start somewhere. Unfortunately, it often requires a journey to the brink of death before people drop the sheer curtain behind which their joy of life is hidden.

*Sunday December 31st 2000,
Happy New Year!*

*"Buffalo Scrotum: Once contained the seeds of life and the future of the herd, now you can use it as a waste receptacle for your car."*

Actual quote from a tag in a gift shop in downtown Orlando.

I've come to a local (disgustingly sterile and contrived) coffee shop to write while CL and her mother sleep in. If the above quote is not enough to convince you of the depravity of contemporary society and its fundamental detachment from the source of all life, then you might as well wipe your ass with what's left of this book, because nothing else I say will do you any good. If the fact that some idiot chooses to profit from the desecration of another of nature's creatures does not convince you to act to save your own skin, then nothing will.

I know, I know… This is where you say, "But look, this sort of thing has been going on forever. There have always been negative members of society, including those who desecrate animals, so get off your high horse. Besides, you're being too naïve. Mankind will act to preserve itself, if and when the need arises. So crawl back into your hole Chicken Little and leave us alone." To which I respond, "True, but at no other time in history has the need to act been more urgent. The combined effects of our recent technological advances, the globalization of economies, and exponential population growth, are leading to a tremendous acceleration of the pace of human evolution. And unless we act intelligently and collectively to evolve in a positive fashion, we will soon slam into a brick wall, the result of which will be catastrophic."

There is a family sitting at the next table debating the difference between spring rolls and egg rolls. No wonder I write. Does anyone, anywhere, actually have real conversations anymore? What are you so afraid of? Do you have to be physically digging yourself out of the rubble of your crumbled world before you grasp the notion of acting on Life? Do you consider yourself safe as long as no one cracks the façade? I once heard this saying:

> *"When light is cast on the pig sty of a man's life,*
> *which do you think he'll condemn first,*
> *the pig sty he wallows in, or the light that reveals it?"*

Condemn me if you like, but all I am trying to do is shed some light on the fact that the reality behind what so many call a life is a pig sty. Wallow if you want. Heed me or ignore me as you see fit. But do not cry when your house of cards comes tumbling down and you have to *act* to survive.

We are but a mere fragment of a finite global ecosystem. Think of us as a relatively highly evolved experiment. It is supremely ignorant to assume the planet exists solely for our benefit or at our discretion. We are but house guests of mother nature. And just as you would expel unruly house guests, so too will nature expel us. And it's not that I'm overly concerned for the well-being of the masses, it's just that I have to live here too. And not only that, but CL will soon be joining the adult world as well. And although I've already warned her of the ignorance she will encounter, it remains my duty as her father to do what I can to help create a more nurturing environment for her. For, as the broken record of my mantra will attest, *we are not meant to live this way!*

The evils of this world is entirely manmade. All evil springs from individual *human* weakness and fear. This is clearly not our natural state, for in nature the weak do not survive. In nature, only those elements conducive to Life are passed on to subsequent generations. Man, in our glorious quest to prove ourselves above nature, has come to embrace weakness. But know this: Weak men feed off the weakness of others, and will do any and everything necessary to propagate this weakness, from crippling your child's natural creativity, to telling ghetto kids there is no life beyond violence and drugs. But you, as a cognitive being, must act on your own volition. It is your self-preservation that must be the motivation for your actions. And this, as some will try to misconstrue, does not require taking from others. Just because you learn, does not mean someone else remains ignorant. Just because you experience a boundless joy for life, does not mean someone else is plagued by despair.

Twice today I have witnessed a mother doting over her child. At first glance one would assume these are the actions of a loving mother. Naturally. But dear mother, your child will learn better if he scrapes his knee falling out of the chair than by you being ever present to catch him. This is also true of man on a global scale, where I am playing the doting mother and can see that man is about to fall out of his chair in a big way. The only problem with the latter scenario is that when you fall, you will in all likelihood take me with you. I have talked to others who also believe a correction is coming, who say only those with the fundamental desire to live will survive, thus abiding the natural law. Because all the money in the world, or fancy cars or clothes or gadgets or country club memberships or contrived blissful ignorance, will not save those who lack the desire to survive.

At the core of each of us is not only the seed kernel of Life, but also the subconscious desire, and resultant capacity, to preserve it. So when I seem to speak poorly of you, it is the external creature that envelopes your True Self I'm talking to, not the gloriously radiant being inside. You may be loathsome on the surface, but deep down, where you think no one else can see (and where maybe you stopped looking long ago), is an intelligent, joyful, and wonderfully alive human being to whom I offer my undieing devotion.

Ultimately, Life will prevail. There is no amount of political corruption or white collar crime or environmental catastrophe or mindless pursuit of profit by any means, that can destroy Life. If mankind were to eradicate itself by nuclear holocaust, then the cockroach would be the pinnacle of evolution. Evolution as we know it would be set back a few billion years, but would simply start over. The Grand Experiment. And maybe a few billion years from now I will be sitting here again, writing the same stale drivel again, imploring my new breed of fellow being to act towards their own preservation. But that is not likely. Nature will not make the same mistake twice. This is our shot. This is our time. It's fourth and goal in the closing seconds of the Super Bowl and you're the quarterback. It's up to you to win or lose the game. Will you act? Will you realize the glory for which you were created? Will you make your fans proud? Or will you go weak in the knees and fumble? I am the center, I am handing you the ball. What are you going to do with it? We are all counting on you. Our lives depend on your success. Good luck my friend, and God bless.

*Tuesday January 2nd 2001*

Have you noticed that we seem to be moving further and further away from self-reliance? We have no idea how to heed our own bodies and cling to whatever our doctors tell us. We have no idea how to work on our own automobiles and depend on the advice of an "honest" mechanic. We have lost all notion of how to deal with our fellow man and hire sharks in suits to do our dirty work. More and more, at almost every segment of our daily lives, we look to someone else to fulfill our needs.

The one constant I can claim is that for most of my adult life I have worked at being as self-reliant as possible. This is why I drive a '62 Ford pick-up and try to learn and do as many different things as I can. It's also why I can claim to have a certain level of understanding of how people, and ultimately society, tick. I know my life depends on both you and I functioning in as advanced a manner as possible, and if you can't see how to make that happen, then I at least have to share my ideas on the subject. In the end, whether I possess a Doctorate in Anthropology or a buzz from too much Guinness, it is up to you to determine how you feel about what I say.

There are those who consider themselves learned in such matters, who point to an imaginary tendency for weakness, which they consider fundamental to "human nature". You are of course free to think of yourself in any way you choose, but goddamn you if you try and teach this to others. One of these days, when you're being honest with yourself, compare your notion of human nature to the religious concept of original sin. What you will find is that these are both excuses for the weak, not Truths in any sense of the word. Just because we continue to pass on a series of socially fabricated frailties to our offspring, does not mean they would develop the same notions if not for our cramming them down their throats.

*Wednesday January 3rd 2001*

There's an old lady who lives across the street from my dad, who literally regrets waking up every morning. She is always saying, "I wish the good lord would take me home. I wish I could just die." Can you imagine the insufferable pain this lady must feel? Can you imagine the havoc she must be wreaking on her body and soul? Does this sound like an unusual case? I'm sorry, but many feel the same to some degree. They seem to believe a fear of death somehow constitutes a joy for living. But fear is fear and joy is joy. The two are diametrically opposed. And fear could not exist if not for the vacuum created from the absence of joy, just as evil could not exist if not for the vacuum created from the absence of good. I once put it like this:

> **"Where there is no light,
> there is darkness"**

It is not true that where there is no darkness there is light. Light is the tangible, the measurable. Darkness is merely the absence of light, a void, a vacuum. Light is that which is positive, darkness is that which literally does not exist. Your religions have only served to deify the darkness. You succumb to the trappings of an imaginary prince of darkness, in ruthless pursuit of someone, anyone, to blame for your own weakness. But there is no such thing. There is only light and the absence of light. Good and the absence of good. Intelligence and the absence of intelligence. Passion and the absence of passion.

The source of these positives is a radiant golden orb of universal energy at the core of your being. And the manifestation of their opposites is proportional to the extent to which you have lost contact with this orb. To put it in Biblical terms, when God breathed Life into the clay, it was this energy God inserted. It is this energy that leaves you when you die. It comes from the same source that gave life to the dead cat you saw on the side of the road this morning and the tree that got plowed over yesterday ("Future home of your new neighborhood Walgreens.") But unlike the cat and the tree, we also possess the ability to ponder the reason for our existence. The problem is that in our pursuit of self-importance, we have made this pondering infinitely harder than it need be.

*later same day*

Katie Couric is a good example of much of what I find wrong with the world today. It's obvious she possesses a higher than average joy for life, yet she continues to contribute to an amoral industry. And although her show is not as guilty as the one now hosted by the talking head she replaced, it is still driven by the pursuit of ratings at all cost. So death is glorified, weakness is deified, and all our socially fabricated frailties are portrayed nightly in living color. At least that clown Springer has the sense to use an ever devolving base of bottom feeders to spew his filth. But Katie Couric is the positive energy off of which all the others feed.

Look at Tom Brokaw for example. Could you imagine what would happen if Tom Brokaw were to stand up one evening and calmly announce to the camera that he refused to read one more story of death and destruction? This sort of thing may be news, but only to those directly involved. If an anchorperson in Orlando for example, were to come on and say, "It is my tragic duty to tell you of a horrible accident on I-4... The family requests that any financial remembrances be donated to...", instead of such an accident being splattered on TV screens coast to coast, I would not feel such animosity for the media as I do.

But as with all things, the media is not alone. Merchandising of all kinds functions in the exact same way. Profit solely for the sake of profit, with all notion of meaning and purpose lost in the storm. So the participants are left feeling unfulfilled and assume that's what life's all about, thereby becoming pawns in their own game. How have we allowed ourselves to get to this point? How much longer do we think we can survive such a vicious cycle of self-deception and parasitic self-immolation?

We all know money is no substitute for happiness, yet we continue to strive for wealth. We all know plastic surgery and make-up are no substitute for natural beauty, yet we continue to support these billion dollar industries. We all know an over rehearsed confidence and scripted speeches are no substitute for steadfast leadership, yet we elected Clinton to two terms! Would you like to know why this is so?

> **"We have sacrificed the whisper of our own Inner Truths to the din of societal deception."**

We think the nagging voices we all hear are unique to ourselves and cannot possibly be applicable to the real world. We are convinced the precedents are too intertwined, the universal grasp of loathing too strong, and the capacity for human ill too powerful. As a result, we extinguish our own light and fear the resulting darkness. We subdue our own strength and cower in fear at everything else. We freely relinquish our joy and languish in mediocrity until our dieing breath. We have created images of a glorious existence beyond the grave as a pathetic substitute for living gloriously *on earth*. We have no way of knowing what, if anything, awaits us after death, but even if this sort of heaven were real, that is no excuse for squandering the life with which we have been blessed, and the only existence of which we can be certain.

So let those of us who want to dance, dance. And those of us who choose to revel in life, live as we will. And when we both stand before God, I will stand proud, brilliant, and beautiful, and you can swoon on your quivering knees. Then God and I will have the last laugh.

> *On the drive from Springfield to South Padre',*
> *with the journal open on the seat beside me...*

Noel Arkansas: Cliffs over Hwy 59, frozen waterfall.

10 year old girl in the back of a pickup parked on the side of the road, firing a 45 semi-automatic pistol into the woods.

"God's House of Pizza"

"Flick One Pawn"

First night, sleeping in the truck on the good side of the Red River, heard my first wild coyote. Heavenly moon, stars and rustling trees.

Drove through Nacogdoches Texas, of *Big Jake* fame.

"Prison area, do not pick up hitchhikers."

Napping, 2:05 PM just south of Houston, startled awake by a dream of her.

Spiritual renewal center on 77.

I can see the Body of Christ out my driver's side window.

> *Monday January 8th 2001 6:45 PM,*
> *Denny's on 77 just outside Corpus Christi*

I've been on the road for 35 hours and it's beginning to show. My boxers smell, I'm a bit chaffed, and I'm not really sure of my presentable'ness. I'm trying to find my brilliant biologist friend (who we will call BBF), who supposedly flew into Corpus at midnight. Hopefully she's already at the apartment. There's a slight possibility I may push myself to get there tonight, which would be just before 11:00 PM. Last night I slept on the south bank of the Red River and would really freak if tonight I were on the beach. Either way, tomorrow my toes will be in the sand, I will drink a beer at a beachside patio, and get my first official taste of being a "Winter Texan."

## Saturday January 13th 2001

So far my visit to South Padre' has been totally surreal. Right now I'm sitting on top of a trash heap at the Brownsville municipal dump (BBF is looking for some kind of bird that apparently can only be found here), watching half a dozen Hispanic kids jumping on a trampoline in their backyard a hundred yards away.

We spent yesterday afternoon at our very own impromptu nude beach. We drank Bloody Mary's, painted each other's tummies, and collected shells in the raw. The drive back was phenomenal. To get there we had driven north out of town about 12 miles down the beach. We kept thinking we'd come to a section designated "clothing optional", but instead the whole route was crowded with cellulite baking retirees and fishermen. We finally just parked the truck, shimmied over a big dune into like a dune valley, and dropped trou.

Driving back there were only two other cars the whole way. The tide was coming in and the waves were all churned and frothy. Cruising in my sweet old truck down 12 miles of secluded beach at dusk, it was like that moment was all there was. If not for the litter, I could have almost pretended no one else existed.

## Wednesday January 17th 2001

Yesterday I read *Here Among the Gods* to BBF and was amazed at how similar it sounded to the works of a philosopher she is reading. I've also met a phenomenal woman who owns the local health food store, who just the other day was quoting a handful of higher thinking authors. All of this to say there are a great many patterns of thought at work in the world today. Some people feel they have a grasp on one pattern, some another. Some believe the world is moved by muscle and not the mind, and therefore generally tend to forgo the necessity for thought altogether. Some feel insignificant in the limitless ocean of ideas and barely dip in more than a big toe.

I'm having one of those mornings where if I could crack open my skull and share an illuminated projection of my thoughts, then we could both analyze them and hopefully both benefit. It's difficult for the pen to move, because as fast as the hand can share one thing, the big bully brain is trying to force in something else. I've been having a few thoughts that seem relevant, perhaps the most significant being the phenomenon of human consciousness in evolutionary terms. I used to think of evolution as a continuous progression towards theoretical perfection, but this implies a goal or destination, which would in turn infer a road map, which would seemingly indicate a driver with some notion of how to get where we're going. In other words, if this notion of evolution were correct, then there would be some theoretically perfect something pulling us towards it. While in purely abstract terms this may be a concept a few can grasp, it is more correct to say evolution is a continual progression *away* from imperfection. And even more correct to simply say evolution is continual progression, which could be further boiled down to say "life is progression."

Movement. Change. BBF has helped me to realize that evolution is largely experimental. The key to understanding any underlying guiding force is Life itself. An organism may develop any trait imaginable, but if that trait does not prove conducive to Life, then that particular experiment will not survive. People have tried to convince me that evolution is *purely* experimental and that everything around us is merely a matter of happenstance. While the billions of metamorphoses over the millennia were experimental at the time, their continued existence is not. And the intricately interwoven ecosystem we all now know and love, most certainly is not. And with this in mind, I can more adamantly state that ***our*** existence is not merely happenstance either.

And this is where human consciousness comes in.

For this exercise, try to envision the overall time span of human existence. Somewhere along the line, man evolved conscious awareness, which we wield as the gilded crown of our superiority. We have even gone so far as to create god in our own image and grant ourselves dominion over the earth. While your consciousness may give you an edge, this does not relieve you of the responsibility of *choosing* how to use it. If we exercise our conscious awareness in a manner conducive to Life we will retain it, but if in our high and mighty ignorance we continue to trample Life, we will eventually devolve to the base mentality of cattle.

Our present position in the hierarchy of life on this planet was won, not by brute force and annihilation, but by the meticulous advancement of individual positive traits. At some point we began to take our mental superiority for granted and began using it in a manner decidedly *not* conducive to Life. In our inability to see the scope of human existence beyond our own, we wrongly assume our contemporary weaknesses (even those spanning thousands of years) are something we can do nothing about. But I assure you that the slow, yet entirely methodical, hand of evolution will weed out our weaknesses as surely as the Neanderthal.

A new friend (let's call him Padre' Fred, or PF for short) says all any of us can do is follow our own path, without being judgmental of others. I believe this is true, but only for those who think of life in such terms. The vast majority of people seem to think of life as some cruel joke or inexplicable struggle, which completely undermines the notion of life on a path, and thus renders moot the practice of not being judgmental. Every single action of every single one of us is intricately intertwined and affects everyone else in ways we will never be able to fully comprehend. Therefore, if your actions are not conducive to Life, then yes I will be judgmental of that fact, at least to the extent required to protect my own existence.

*Thursday January 18th 8:00 AM*

Last night I dreamt I was an Old West landowner, a Ben Cartwright kind of character. I even remember having a similarly proud demeanor and two sons. The local paper ran a story saying I had found evidence of gold on my property. The dream began with a family of outlaws riding out to declare they were taking my land. They said they would spare our lives if we signed over the deed and left peacefully. I know there were strong words spoken and I made it clear I was not intimidated by them, but I agreed to their demands anyway. Then the man decided (I suppose out of celebration) to go in my room and have sex with his woman. I remember standing on the porch of the house and catching a peripheral glimpse of a townsperson running over the hill to my left. Within seconds there was a horde of people swarming over the hill. They were not stopping, but were slamming into the house as if the clues to the gold's whereabouts could be found in its splintered remains. When they learned the new owner was holed-up in the bedroom, they began to clamor about the walls of the room like bees on a hive. After a moment I yelled "Quiet!" at the top of my lungs and everyone, both inside and outside the house, turned to look at me.

"First let me tell you the story in the paper is not entirely untrue", I said with a sheepish grin. The crowd squirmed a little but for the most part remained silent. "We found evidence of gold in a clump of dirt but I cannot tell you where we dug up the clump, because when we found it, it was lodged in the blade of the plow."

Then I awoke from my dream but for some reason continued the dialogue as if I were really in that situation. I remember saying we would form a corporation of all the townspeople and mine the gold as such. That both the land on which the gold was found and the gold itself would be placed in public trust. And that the profits from the mine would not be squandered to fatten our bellies or put silk robes on our backs, but would serve to enrich the lives of everyone in much more meaningful ways, and also to enrich the lives of the poor (meaning the poor in fact, not in spirit.)

Maybe somewhere in this plowed field of words there is a clump that contains evidence of gold. All I can do is try to get the words down on paper. After that, we have to mine the field together.

What I do know is that material possessions are of little value once one's basic needs have been met. That an off-brand sheet will keep your legs just as warm as a name-brand sheet. That a '62 Ford pickup will get you to the art supply store just as well as a Jaguar. The only proper use of excess material gain is to help meet the basic needs of those with less, so they can relax long enough to view their destiny. One of the positive aspects of contemporary Western society is that we have reached a capacity for providing the basic needs for everyone, whether we choose to do so or not. What we must get beyond is the poverty mentality (to covet what we do not have) and the wealth mentality (to falsely substantiate self-worth through material hoarding.) Neither practice is conducive to Life, and both only serve to perpetuate the other. Neither feeds the soul or enriches the self.

Postscript: Isn't it funny how in the dream, once the townspeople decided to listen to reason and work together, the outlaws ceased to be of any significance? The same would work in society, but we seem to enjoy the excitement of criminal activity. Why else do you think we deify its existence?

*Sunday January 21st 8:00 AM*

This morning I touched the origins of life on Earth, held it in the palm of my hands. Literally. Suddenly, years of attempting to understand interconnectedness became perfectly clear. If it's not possible for you to envision tangible interconnectedness, then think of it as the air you breathe. Breathing is the process by which we (our bodies) take in oxygen so that we (that which is aware of itself and of reading these words) can remain alive. But imagine instead of breathing being merely a simple biological process of oxygen exchange, that this were the very act of interconnectedness itself.

I'm using this as a simple example of another profound Truth, in hopes that those who have attempted to remove themselves from the process may grasp some notion of what I'm saying. Beware the tendency to make things too complicated, as this is merely our feeble brain attempting to substantiate its sense of self-importance by trying to work too hard. It's almost as dangerous as trying to oversimplify things, which is merely our brain thanking us for its sense of self-importance by trying to make us think it understands something. When all the while, the only way to ever Know anything is to simply let go of your illusion of being removed from it. When you accept that you are simply a pea in the soup of Life, then you will understand all those things you no longer consider yourself separate from.

So while our Western doctors and scientists amuse themselves by pretending to have some higher grasp on the mechanics of life, and our Eastern spiritualists and philosophers amuse themselves by pretending to have some grasp on the fluidity of life (the gas in the engine if you will), what we should be doing is trying to understand what lies beneath both of these. But there is a practical reason why man evolved consciousness, which is what caused us to consider ourselves as separate in the first place, which in turn set us on this insane mindfuck of trying to understand the world we now consider ourselves as separate from.

In truth, it is not our consciousness that is separate from nature, but the choices we make with it. Beyond this, even the choices we make that are not conducive to Life are still a part of evolution, even if it means our eventual self-destruction. We look around at our environmental atrocities and some of us think we are destroying the planet, but what we are really doing is destroying ourselves. Some random act of evolutionary experimentation caused us to become self-aware. We then used this self-awareness to trick ourselves into thinking we were somehow separate from the natural world around us and in us.

Life, the ebb and flow of energies throughout the Universe, is a wondrous folly of experimentation. Evolution is the process by which these experiments either succeed or fail. Everything around us is the accumulative result of unknown gazillions of such experiments. Everything is connected because it has all evolved together. There is no one living thing on the planet that simply popped into being and can somehow exist separate from all the other living things around it. Man is merely one more "thing" that has evolved in this wondrous pot of stew we call Earth. But man evolved a distinctly unique trait, and that is the capacity to *choose* between acting in a manner conducive to our own existence or not. And this, my friends, represents an extraordinary leap of faith in the process of evolution.

When the experiment of fish evolved the capacity to crawl on land, all of the trillions of interconnected molecular processes by which this experiment occurred were all individually gauged by their respective conducivity to Life. Sure, billions upon billions of little critters died before one of them succeeded, but all the while it was the life of the infinitesimally altered subsequent generation that fueled the entire process. Somewhere along the way, one of these subsequent generations developed the capacity to choose to act. No longer was the pursuit of life a trial and error process. Instead of being forced to work through the physical manifestations of evolutionary experimentation, man evolved a miraculous shortcut by which we could *conceive of* the evolutionary process! The pursuit of life was advanced beyond the gut wrenchingly slow physical process to the instantaneous theoretical process. As a result, we have not only domesticated the horse, but have created hundreds of distinct breeds in the process. If these had been left to natural selection, they would have taken millions of years to occur, if they would have ever occurred at all.

The course of human history can be seen within the context of evolution as well. We have reached a point where the combined impact of our individual actions is of epic proportion. The urgency I feel in writing this book is fueled by a vision of mankind being in a race against time. Our tremendous technological advances over the past century and a half, coupled with exponential population growth, places a greater array of tools by which the theoretic processes of evolution can be manifested into the hands of a greater number of people. And unless we employ our consciousness to the specific task of supporting Life, then our fate can only be death.

There are those among us who feel so separate from Life that they systematically (albeit most often subconsciously) choose to act for death. One common socially fabricated frailty is to consider ourselves as not only separate from the natural world, but also separate from our fellow humans as well. As a result, we are left feeling afraid and confused, like a gilled creature floundering in the last remnants of a tidal pool. This fear becomes so intense it causes us to believe that if we kill or otherwise maim the life forces we see as outside of ourselves, we somehow inflate our own. All this to the point where a great deal of the very structure of society serves no purpose but to blind our children to the gift of Life. Throw an extra seventy-five million or so logs onto this fire every year, and eventually the flames are going to consume everything in their wake.

All I am trying to do is illuminate a few minds to the fact that our survival as a species is purely a matter of choice. One of the major stumbling blocks in our past social development was the lack of communication. As seeing ourselves as separate from that other tribe (nation, race, social caste, etc.), we felt that destroying it would somehow benefit our own. But now global communication is so advanced that we not only have the capacity to understand one another, but to teach one another as well. Instead of our technologies aiding the confusion, separation, and death, they can aid the understanding, cohesion, and life, in ways inconceivable to past societies, both East and West.

And what was it I held in my hands this morning that seems to have made such an impact? Sand. The finest of sand at the edge of the incoming tide. BBF and I were digging for clams in the stretch of beach that remains saturated from the lapping waves. We had used a plastic cup to dig a hole about the size of a kid's shoe box, when I decided to reach in and get a scoop with my hand. Imagine a small pit at the edge of the water, with sand so fine that the walls are constantly collapsing, and the bottom of the pit is full of water and sediment. When I reached in I quickly jerked my hand back because I felt a noticeable electric shock.

Apparently salt dissolves in water to produce positively charged sodium ions and negatively charged chlorine ions, which explains the slight charge. Where the ocean meets land you have all the necessary ingredients for life: Oxygen, water, and sunlight, which are all kept stirred up by the gentle motion of the waves. It has been theorized that the building blocks of life forming amino acids were such charged ions bonded to inversely charged surfaces, although there is little consensus as to what these surfaces may have been. Given this morning's revelation, I am lead to believe these surfaces were the various silicates that can found in sand. It's difficult to explain, but for that one brief moment I honestly felt as if I were kneeling in the very cradle of (aerobic) life on Earth.

# ᛫ Book III ᛫

*Monday January 22nd 2001*

Okay folks, it's time to kick this thing into high gear. There have been several new developments in the adventure over the last few days. Friday, after realizing I had just broken my last twenty, I rode my bike around the island to jot down the names and numbers of architects with projects under construction. (Have I mentioned that I'm an architect? Specifically, a CAD literate architect with highly marketable construction documentation skills?) I got a positive response on my very first call, from an architect from Harlingen who said he had a hotel project he needed to farm out. He drove out to the island on Saturday, which is when I had to confess I didn't have a computer. "No problem", he said, and proceeded to buy me a laptop! To top it all off he gave me a cash advance because I also confessed that I was broke, as usual.

*Wednesday January 24th 2001*

I absolutely cannot believe how incredible life is right now. I'm sitting cross-legged on the daybed in my tiny efficiency apartment on South Padre', working on the hotel on my brand new laptop. I can look out the window to my left and see the dunes, beyond which is the beach and the Gulf of Mexico. There is a huge Monarch butterfly fluttering around the front yard. I tell ya', nothing is finer on the planet. I had to say a quick prayer a moment ago to express my appreciation and to ask that any lingering bad karma doesn't blow it all.

## Tuesday January 30th 2001

It's 11 o'clock at night and for some reason I can't sleep. Maybe it was the laptop calling my name, or maybe I'm just lonely. Maybe I feel there's so much to be done, leaving room for little else, including sleep, or maybe I'm just lonely. It could be the king sized Hershey bar I ate about 9:30, or maybe I'm just lonely. Of all the ills that plague man, the most common is the easiest to solve and the most overlooked. But I would rather be alone than surrounded by non-intimate acquaintances. There are other things afoot too. Deep dark caverns of a soul that must be searched. Crevices where no man has trod in decades. I must look in these places to find the skeletal remains of the me's that have come before, in order to understand the me I am now. Or maybe I'm just lonely.

## Sunday February 4th 2001

There have been many millennia of man before us. There have been dreamers and destroyers of dreams, who have lived and died, fought and loved, hoped and cried. Many besides ourselves have wanted a life different from their own, have dreamed of a reality outside of their grasp. All societies considered themselves to be the pinnacle of societal evolution at the time of their own existence. How many people who lived a thousand years ago longed to end poverty or political corruption or senseless human strife or mediocrity? Much of what we have been taught about history has been tainted to better the position of whomever was doing the teaching, but what about the people who actually lived it? Were they able to see into the future and imagine anything close to what we are today? Did they have any tools available for a deeper insight into life than our own? Did their brain or heart somehow function in a manner different from ours?

I will tell you what I believe. I believe that for the vast majority of human existence, life was ruled by superstition. Anything not understood was treated with doubt and suspicion. And the deeper the misunderstanding, the more likely the thing in question was to be either worshiped or reviled. Thunder, for no better reason than a lack of scientific knowledge of its origin, was labeled a god. Native Americans, for no better reason than European settlers' inability to appreciate their social structure, were labeled as savages and wiped off the face of the Earth.

We have spent eons cowering behind veils of doubt and suspicion. It has become so engrained in our psyche that millions have died in battles waged over little else. Men hoard tons of senseless possessions, drink oceans of liquor, and defile everything in their wake, to try and squelch the screams of doubt and suspicion in the far dark corners of their souls. Instead of walking into the Light, they try and drag everyone else into the darkness with them.

We live in a time when communication has finally reached the point where, if we wanted, we could make it possible for most of us to fight against the pull into that dark cave. So many before us were without the tools necessary and thus entered unwittingly and died in utter darkness. The screamers in the caves have given their tactics many fancy and colorful names in order to entice unsuspecting victims. Who wouldn't take a stab at eight years of being the most powerful man on the planet, replete with gratuitous oral sex, in exchange for simply taking a few steps into the darkness? "Come on, just a few steps won't hurt. Look at all the hard work you put in at Oxford. You deserve a break today." Even I would be tempted by such a prospect. But before you know it, your entire life is nothing but a lie. You have lost all notion of the Light and are engulfed in darkness. Your stature has been replaced with shoulder pads, your passion with scripted speeches, your guidance with political expediency, and respect with mimicry. The ones who came before, the ones who lured you into the cave, have succeeded in their quest and you have failed in yours. You have sold your soul, and for what? In the end what have you gained? Do you feel any more comfortable inside your own skin than you did before? Of course not, how could you? When all you do is flee the meaningful, the meaningless is all you will find.

I'm not sure why I enjoy picking on Clinton so much, he couldn't help it. Imagine if you were a poor boy from Arkansas, with women and celebrities throwing themselves at you. You've got men in expensive suits handing you suitcases full of cash and guaranteeing you perks out the ass. What would you have done differently? Hell yeah, take the money, blow jobs, and expensive haircuts, and tell humanity to shove it. Don't get me wrong, I think he started out with good intention, like in junior high, but to quote the little guy, "Once you start down the dark path, forever will it dominate your destiny."

But I'm rambling again, aren't I? My morning tea has pulled me out of Alpha mode and my mind is racing in Beta. I'm trying too hard and the result is my completely losing track of what I wanted to say. I was comparing the impact that our current capacity for communication has on our lives, versus the impact that the lack of communication had on the lives of previous generations. The most important questions are how have we dragged the superstitions created in those past eras into our own, and what are we going to do about it? That is why we all need to take a collective breath, slow our insanely hectic pace, and reconsider every single aspect of our existence. From the foundations of our social structure and economies, to our various religions, traditions, and beliefs. Hopefully, after we take the first breath we will want to take another. Then we could really cleave open our souls and reexamine our past misunderstandings, in hopes of paving the way to a better future for us all.

Do we even want a future? Is it only me who wants a better life for mankind? Am I the only person who wants to end the senselessness, simply because it is senseless not to? Is the mind inside my head the only mind with the capacity to envision a better life for us all? A more cohesive version of each of the fragments disseminated above? Am I the only person who envisions the lives of future generations and knows we can make those lives better, if for no other reason than just to prove we can?

No, of course I'm not. But I will tell you what I am. I am one man with one voice. I am a man trying to live his life like everyone else. And, like everyone else, I have been tricked into the darkness. Will I stumble into the cave again? I would like to stand atop a mountain and scream an emphatic "NO!" for all the world to hear, but even I wouldn't believe me. But neither will I overly berate myself when I once again stand in the Light.

I have a pet peeve. When I'm talking with someone and they are relating something they think may be over my head and ask, "Do you understand?" I just hate that. But since we have no way of directly communicating, I will ask, "Do you understand?" Does all this sound like new age hocus-pocus? I can imagine you're chuckling now, but tonight when you're lying in bed you will rethink the matter. I can even guarantee that if Clinton were to read these words he would say, "My god, how did he know that's how I feel inside?!? Is he a mind reader? A sorcerer?" Would you like to know how I know these things? *Because on the inside we are all the same!*

We all have our own array of beliefs and traditions. We all have our own set of data indices by which we try to sort the world around us. You may be high on crack just as I am high on self-righteousness. You may think your million bucks is more significant than the fifty just loaned to me by a dear friend. But on the inside we are all the same. We all evolved from the same pool. It is not money or fame or power that causes our bodies to live and think and shit, it is Life.

And Life, by its very nature, craves that which is conducive to its existence. And the one distinction I make in all I espouse is to discern between that which is conducive to Life and that which is not. Inner Peace is conducive to Life, insanity is not. Peace within a society and between societies is conducive to Life, crime and war are not. A healthy economic structure in which everyone succeeds or fails based on their own input and initiative is conducive to Life, hoarding and suppression are not. Ecological interaction that maintains the sanctity of nature is conducive to Life, strip mining is not. A government that functions as an umbrella of protection from viable threats is conducive to Life, one driven by lobbyists and campaign contributions is not.

Either you choose Life or you don't. But do not try to fool yourself by using cutesy phrases to hide what it is you're really after. Like the drunk who calls alcohol "refreshment", or the sexual deviant who calls porn "harmless", if you are not after Life, then what you are really after is death. There is no middle ground. There is no "little war" or "minor corruption". There is only war or peace, corruption or integrity, Life or death.

I have to stop a moment however, and extend due respect to the death mongers. They have been far more successful over the last few thousand years than the rest of us. For whatever reason, yours seems to be the majority opinion. Even when each and every one of you secretly crave Life at your core, you have succeeded in defeating even yourselves, so that your ways prevail. I have to hand it to you. If only I could finagle such a strategy. How do you think it's possible your kind have thrived while my kind have suffered?

We all have trials and tribulations, some as a consequence of our own actions, some wrought by others. Many of us have been shown the woman of our dreams, only to have her held at a cruel distance. But are these simply lessons to be learned? Is suffering required to help us appreciate comfort? Have so many evils occurred throughout history at the hands of those who choose death, so that those of us who choose Life would do so more adamantly? Therein lies the question: Do we? Do we crave peace because we have known the horrors of war? Do we crave feast because we have endured the pangs of famine? Do we crave creativity because we have smelt the putrid stench of mediocrity?

Of course not. And why not you ask? Is it because we are ignorant? Is it because there is a weakness engrained in human nature? Is it because we are all sinners doomed to an existence of loathing in exchange for life after death? No, it is not. All of these things, everything that has happened throughout the entire course of human history, were simply evolutionary experiments.

Evolution is the process by which these experiments are sorted by one simple rule: Conducive to Life or not conducive to Life. In nature these decisions are made automatically. The forces of nature determine what will stay and what will go, not the individual plant or animal in question. In nature, Life prevails because Life is all there is. A plant or animal cannot act to its own detriment, that would be contrary to every flicker of energy in every cell of its being.

Unfortunately however, man somehow evolved the capacity to choose, and over the years have made more than our fair share of mistakes. The reason why those seeking death have always appeared successful is simply because while they were enjoying their follies of death, the biological entities which were themselves were refusing to let go of Life. Hitler had to ultimately stick a gun to his head, because even at the height of his death mongering his body refused to die on its own. He had to exercise the physical choice of overriding his body's own desire to live. How ironic. What the Hitlers of the world have always failed to realize is that while their minds may have been cowering in a dark cave, their bodies – every cell of their bodies - were screaming for Life. While they were exercising their conscious choices of death, their Universal Subconscious remained focused on Life. Their actions were in vain the entire time. Corrupt politicians and corporate executives may be able to kill off a few of us, or maim an entire generation's belief system, but they can't get us all. Their own bodies won't allow it. All the pain and suffering has been for naught. As horrendous as it was at the time, and continues to be, it has always been to no avail...

Until now.

Now we live in an era when those who choose death can do so on a global scale. And those who know how to trick others into the cave can do so in far greater numbers. Everything about contemporary society, from the Internet to nuclear weapons, from our understanding of psychology to all you can eat buffets, from our poor excuse of a government to our poor excuse of an educational system, everything now makes it possible for those who choose death to actually win. Never before have so many tools been at their disposal. Never before has so much of what goes into the makings of a society been so readily available to the wrong people.

And I'm not just talking about the possibility of Saddam Hussein getting his hands on a few nukes, I'm talking about everything. From the fact that giving Coke to a child sets them up for addictive tendencies later in life, to the fact that raping the environment for the aluminum in the disposable can represents a huge link in the chain of global neglect. From the fact that Madison Avenue only exists because you need to be told what's hip, to the fact that there is even such a concept as hip. From the existence of Jerry Springer, who feeds on an ever devolving base of ignorance, to the existence of the NFL, which feeds on your disregard for your own inner hero. When you combine all of these things, and when you begin to see them for what they really are, you begin to understand that death is finally possible. Life has been undermined to the point where it is almost as expendable as a used razor.

So the question for all of us becomes, how close to our own death are we willing to creep before we decide we want to live? How far down the path of self-destruction do we travel before we decide to turn back? How deep into the cave do we go before we once again crawl towards the Light? And I'm not talking to some fictional character we conveniently label as society, but to you. I'm not talking to Bill Clinton the President, I am talking to Bill Clinton the man. I am talking to every single person reading these words this very second. When are *you* going to start choosing Life?

With every single thing you do, every breath, every spoonful of food, every thought, and every motivation. From the big things like how you earn your living and raise your children, to the small things like what type of music you listen to. All of your beliefs, motivations and desires. Your attitudes toward sex, society, God, your fellow man, and yourself. Your own sense of beauty, creativity and intelligence, and your acceptance or denial of these things in others. With every aspect of your life, both physical and metaphysical, you have to make the choice between Life or death. And *you* have to make the choice, no one can do it for you.

But the first question to ask is do you want to live? I started to say if the answer were no, then you should at least muster the decency to remove yourself from the equation, but instead I will let you in on a little secret. It is impossible for you to honestly answer no to this question. Whatever it is rattling around inside your head that sounds like a no, take it out and analyze it objectively. What you will undoubtedly find is that it was placed there by someone else. Were you abused as a child, neglected by your father, fondled by Uncle John? Were you constantly berated by an overbearing teacher or left to fend for yourself in the gutter? Were you an accident of ejaculation and therefore treated as such your entire life? Do you see yourself as somehow less than or unworthy of the world around you? Are you not starting to see a common thread here?

All of these things were dictated by forces outside of your skin during a period of your life over which you had absolutely no control, and have no bearing whatsoever on what you choose to be within your own skin now.

Uncle John? Fuck'im. Your father? Fuck'im. The teacher? You guessed it, fuck him too. All of these people were simply bipedal hominids with an evolved consciousness that saddled them with not only the capacity but also the resultant responsibility to make decisions, which led to their own fear and disbelief in their ability to do so. They thought that by somehow corrupting the beautiful child that was once yourself, they could somehow, if not pull themselves out of the cave, at least have a little company. But *you* had to decide to join them. And no matter how young you were when you made the choice, even while in infancy, you still have the power to change. By the way, 99.99% of us were accidents of ejaculation, so you'll just have to get over that ploy. Regardless of the biological facts of your creation, you were created. You are here. Deal with it.

I've been writing (and editing on the fly, thanks to my new laptop) for the past 5 hours. I've had tea, yogurt, and just downed a sandwich for lunch. I've thought about everything I wanted to say, and have hopefully said it sufficiently for you to understand and appreciate. If not, go sit under a tree for a couple of hours and maybe it will come to you. Better yet, get outta' Dodge and go camp out under a tree for a few days.

Going through the back of my mind are thoughts of all the people who will never read this book, and of those who do, will consider it holier-than-thou mumbo jumbo. I know I do not hold all the answers. I know even if I did, many of you would not care to listen. Yet the fact remains, too much of what exists in the world today exists only to serve those who are in the cave.

*Tuesday February 6th 2001 7:26 AM*

## "Unification Theory"

If you've never had the opportunity to watch the sunrise over the ocean, I definitely recommend moving it closer to the top of your list. There is something about the combination of the soft lull of the surf and the brilliant fire of the sun shattering the sky like a cheap windshield, that sends the soul soaring. If you're the sort to enjoy quiet contemplation, there are few places finer. This morning, as I crested the dunes in front of my apartment and upon my first glimpse of the beach, the above phrase appeared to me as clearly as if it were flashing on a billboard. Have you ever been struck with a concept and almost immediately felt you understood it completely, even if you weren't privy to all the details? That's what this was.

*Friday March 2nd 2001*

I swear I just clicked on the TV and heard this actual statement on a national morning news program: "As we do every week, we convene a morning roundtable to discuss the latest happenings on Survivor." Convene a morning roundtable to discuss a goddamn TV show?!? Holy crap, I think I'll just forget this whole book idea and let you people go on over the cliff by yourselves. I'll be damned if I waste a moment's effort trying to save anyone who treats a "reality" television show as something of substance and our current sociopolitical structure as an unavoidable fact of life.

*later same day*

CL and I were hanging out on the beach the other day and I was telling her about the three levels of influencing society. The first and most common is influencing *what* people think. Madison Avenue is a perfect example of this. By making people feel somehow less complete if they wear anything other than Tommy jeans, they in turn sell tons of Tommy jeans. The second and more laborious is influencing *how* people think. The women's lib movement was a good example of this. The purpose there was to transform entire thought patterns to more equalize women's place in society. The third and nearly impossible is attempting to influence *if* people think. If I want you to get anything at all from this book, it is to realize that you have the power to *choose* to think.

## *Friday March 23rd*

For millions of years, life existed on Earth without humans. As a mental exercise, I want you to try and take humans out of the picture again. Rocks would follow still gravity downhill, plants would still point towards the sun, bees would still make honey, and birds would still fly south for the winter. Everything would have its own particular frequency of consciousness and, as such, would coexist in a measurable hierarchy based on these levels. The dolphin would likely be somewhere close to the top of the heap. The only difference between this imaginary ecosystem and life as we know it, is that all living things would be moved by some inexplicable phenomenon causing it to automatically act in a manner conducive to Life.

Now we have Earth's ecosystem trucking right along without humans. So if everything else would function just fine without us, why did we evolve? And why was it not enough that we evolved bipedal or smooth skinned or with opposable thumbs? Why did we also evolve a frequency of consciousness that has caused us to be self-aware? Why did we evolve the unique capacity to act as something other than a mere patsy to evolution?

## CHOICE

Cut it out, paste it on everything you own, even tattoo it across your chest. Human consciousness evolved *precisely* so some life form could act based on a conscious decision of whether to live or die, versus merely going through the motions required to remain animated. Here's another:

## WILL AND INTENT

Of far greater import than even the capacity to choose, is the proper employment of will and intent. Before you can realize the power of unfettered will and intent (the true power of human subconsciousness), you must first fully choose Life. The latter supersedes the former. Everything has some degree of consciousness, there are other life forms that exercise varying degrees of choice, but the human mind is the only bundle of chemicals and energy in the known Universe that has evolved the capacity to exercise will and intent.

You have no higher purpose in life than repairing whatever it is inside you that is acting, either consciously or subconsciously, towards anything other than Life. We all contain varying degrees of both: Life and death, love and joy, passion and fear. But until you have a more firm grasp on the positive than the negative, your subconscious will act to manifest negatives in your life. Once the balance of power is firmly entrenched in the positive, not only will your subconscious manifest positives in your life, but you will also realize an abundance of power you will be able to share with the world around you.

Many have relinquished this power to those who consciously act towards death. We have lost sight of the fact that these people are literally powerless in the Universal sense. As a consequence, we have dropped our shield of Universal protection and run in fear from any thug with a gun or politician with a pen.

*Sunday March 25th 2001 8:45 AM*

My daughter and I are in Progresso, Mexico. She is sleeping in and I am writing over breakfast in our hotel restaurant.

I know it must be frustrating when I throw out really off the wall ideas in only a few sentences, like I expect you to just get it or something. But the fact is you *do* get it. The only reason you feel you don't is because you simply find it easier to tell yourself it's over your head than to just think about it. But these Truths are as old as the Universe itself, while your rejection is simply a contemporary byproduct of your own conditioning.

Life is the driving force behind all there is. You see proof of it every day. With everything we try to destroy, no matter the degree, once we stop, Life begins the rebuilding process. If we were to destroy human life and 99.99% of all life on the planet in the process, Life would just shrug its shoulders and start all over. The experiment of human consciousness would be over, time to try something else.

☙

I want to insert something here I originally wrote in the in the Spring of '94:

"One day, four young boys went exploring a creek in search of treasure. Three decided they would form a team and crisscross back and forth, turning over every log and stone. One found a nice shady spot under a willow tree to sit beside the creek. The three went hurriedly about their way scouring the banks and bottom. The one just sat. The three laughed at the one and called him lazy and foolish. The one just sat. As the days passed, the four continued their search. One day as the three were turning over logs, one of them was bitten by a snake and died. The one beneath the willow had spent that day dreaming of a leaf floating along with the soft current. A few days later, as the two were busily flipping rocks, one fell into the water and drowned. The one sitting quietly had spent that day pondering the course of a mighty hawk soaring high above the creek. As more time passed, the lone industrious one paced hurriedly up and down the sides of the creek. He felt he must do the work of three if he were going to find the treasure. Within a few days, as the sun bore down, he was struck with heat exhaustion and died. The passive one continued to sit in the cool shade of the willow tree. He spent his days contemplating the beauty of nature and the joyous wonder of Life. One day towards the end of the season he noticed a shell tumbling along the bottom of the creek. He was amazed with its beauty and bent to pick it up for a closer look. When he opened the shell he was amazed to find a radiant orb of solid gold."

At the core of each of us is a golden orb of untainted (pure) energy that is the font of all our beauty, intelligence, passion and creativity. It is also the point at which we truly communicate with, and are connected to, the world around us. This orb is our Life force. Without it we would be corpses. While we are alive we can do nothing that is ultimately contrary to this force. This orb is also in all things. Our scientists see this as the nucleus of an atom, however it is not matter, but energy. All energy is Life, all Life is energy. We may consciously act in ways contrary to our individual lives, but in the end, Life will prevail.

We live in a world where those who utilize their conscious abilities for evil - anything not conducive to Life - have little to stop them but mindless cattle. Or so they think. They believe that for as long as you simply follow the herd and do as you are told, they will maintain control. So the only real question here is do we continue to pussy-foot around, or do we take a stand once and for all? The longer we avoid the question, the closer we creep to the abyss.

The time has come for a show down.

*Sunday April 1st*

Hey. I am inputting handwritten entries from Book I, and for some reason was struck with the notion of saying hello. I think it has to do with the fact I've had company for the last three weeks straight (CL just went home yesterday) and now I'm bored and lonely and needed someone to talk to. I have the efficiency for another week and am trying to psych myself up to do a lot of writing. I've charted a course for the Grand Canyon from here, but am not exactly sure how that will pan out.

*Saturday April 7th 2001*

I'm at an outdoor music festival in Dripping Springs, Texas, about 20 miles west of Austin. I left Padre' late Thursday and got here just before lunchtime on Friday. I've reached a point with at least the introspective part of the adventure where I just need to let things jell, but still I find myself wanting to write. I am struggling with something, although it's hard to say what. It's easy to speak hypothetically of living, but in the end it's a fairly complex process. I wish I could just figure it all out.

*Saturday April 21st*

The adventure has taken a decidedly different turn. A couple of weeks ago, the idea was to begin the final push towards the Grand Canyon. But at the festival in Dripping Springs, everyone kept telling me about an awesome 18-day folk festival in Kerrville, which is where I am now. Although the festival itself is more than a month away, I decided to come here instead of dragging Louie across three states, just to turn around and come back, because I seriously did not want to miss this thing. I anticipate the energy will be conducive to some serious input, which will be a relief after such a long break. (BTW, have I mentioned I named my truck Louie, after a club on the island?!)

There's been another interesting development. CL's mother has asked me to move to Orlando so we can share a house and expenses, and to be honest, I'm pretty excited about the idea.

### Sunday April 22nd 2001

Yesterday one of the other volunteers and I were talking about religion and spirituality while slinging paint. I was sharing the idea that the answers we seek are not in anything available to be read, including the Bible. That no matter what you read or what you are told, the words mean nothing until you hear them, decipher them, question them, turn them inside out and upside down. Then, and only then, can you take those words into your soul and make them a part of your overall belief system. All any written or spoken word can do is provide some semblance of a guidepost on the road you are attempting to travel. I once put it like this:

> **Enlightenment cannot be found in a book,**
> **For it can neither be written or read.**
> **Enlightenment cannot be found in a prophet,**
> **For it can neither be spoken or heard.**
> **Enlightenment cannot be found,**
> **For it has never been lost.**

Enlightenment in this sense simply means both the desire to want a better life and the intuitive knowledge required to bring it about.

### Saturday April 28th 2001

In the end, everyone just wants to be understood and to experience true intimacy and peace. The cruel joke we all play on ourselves is that, on the inside, we all feel this way. But we are so afraid to appear weak and needy that we don't share our feelings and wind up spending our lives in a desperate struggle, all for nothing.

We evolved initially as a species, then as a people. Over the millennia we have chosen to fragment ourselves to the point where we hardly even know ourselves anymore, much less our neighbors. I believe it is our destiny to resolve this and to discover the life available to us all on the other side. No longer can we afford to act like strangers or to consider ourselves as such. No longer can we afford to go about our own business without concern as to how our actions affect our fellow man or our mother. And we will all come to this conclusion one way or the other, all we can do now is attempt to lessen the blow.

*Saturday May 5th 2001*

Back at Kerrville for another work weekend but most of the crews are overstaffed, so I've snuck off to the kitchen to write. There's been yet another excellent development in the adventure. When I was here two weeks ago I met this man who has a roofing crew in Austin, who hooked me up with an hourly labor gig without my even really having to ask. Then he introduced me to a friend of his who needs a deck built. As it turns out, I'm building a deck and a fence, painting the pool, and remodeling the guest bath. *And* she offered to rent me a room at her house with food included - I am so set! It's hard to imagine how I could have manifested such a wonderful gig, but it is a perfect example nonetheless.

༃

Something's been bouncing around inside my troubled head for a while now, and I think it's finally ready to spill onto the page...

It's odd how attached we all are to our beliefs. No matter who we are, we all tend to stick to people who fit into our particular life pattern. This is true of the rich and poor, black and white, and yes, even hippie and straight. I used to think this was because people prefer having others around with whom they share something in common, but I'm beginning to realize most just don't want to have their beliefs challenged. The other night I was talking with a woman who meditates and consults a "guru". She tried to explain that her meditation was a systematic process of attempting to heal the karma of her past lives, thereby moving closer to the Divine Within. I said the Divine Within was divine regardless and needed only to be revisited, which requires more of a belief than a systematic process. Anyway, what I took away from our conversation was that she's perfectly happy with her process and didn't particularly appreciate my challenging her. By this I mean she's gotten caught up in the process itself, and has since lost sight of what was once supposedly the original goal.

The most important thing in life is to always challenge yourself. Similar to the quest for knowledge, you have to have a firm base to latch onto, but also have to reach for the unknown at the same time. The same is true of your social situation. It's fine to be a hippie, but what about when life calls for interacting with straights? You have to be willing to let go of your preconceived notions, get out of the comfort zone, and get a little on you. You know the old saying "walk a mile in my shoes"? One thing I can say is that I've worn many shoes. As such I have seen inside the lives of many different types of people and have experienced firsthand, if only in small doses, many different social attitudes and belief systems. Most of the things I espouse are applicable to all of these, especially the tendency to stick to our own.

*"Peace to the believer"*, a quote from a fellow Kerrvert who just walked by.

ఎ

For some reason, I was just struck with the dedication for this book. Truth is reality as it exists, with or without our interpretations. Justice is the proper balance required to maintain these Truths. And the essence of "the American way" is the individual freedom to seek these Truths of our own accord.

I've come to a part of the festival grounds called Chapel Hill. It's the crest of a hill about 30 yards in diameter, with a huge old live oak right on top. There's a twig arbor (a semi-circular enclosure built from limbs and sticks) a little less than halfway around the tree. In the center of this, in front of the tree, is what looks like a crude lectern built of heavy timbers. Hanging from a limb of an adjacent tree is a wind chime made of very large diameter metal pipe, which peels with the most spiritually resonate tones I've ever heard. It's still early on Saturday morning and I'm here all alone. The sun is trying to peek through an almost completely overcast sky and I can hear the blended melody of at least a half dozen different types of birds. I can feel a slight tingly sensation in the upper half of my skull, which I attribute to the tangible energy of this place. I want the words to flow now please…

On the ground in front of me I can see the marks I made the last time I was here. There's a small wooden pad by the trunk of the wind chime tree, which I assume is for meditation, where I had allowed myself to go into a low level trance as I placed my hands on the peat covered earth. After a few moments I was rocking gently back and forth, digging my hands deeper into the cool, moist soil as I went. I imagined this as gleaning healing energy from our mother, which is a wonderful thing to imagine. It's nice to be able to conceive of such things as a God, a Savior, Universal Energy, and the healing spirit of a Mother Earth. This is so much healthier than living in doubt and fear. Our personal beliefs are the ultimate force that governs our lives. If you believe in God, then immerse yourself in that belief and let that light be your guide. Do not concern yourself with attempting to convert others. If you believe in meditation and working through the karma of past lives, then go with that. Revel in it and live it. If you believe laying naked in the grass infuses your body with healing energy, then by god lay naked in the grass as often as you can. The only real trick is to *believe*. Then, just when you think you firmly and unequivocally believe, let go of that belief. Listen to the thoughts of others. Listen to their ideas and share your own with them. Do not berate, chide or otherwise belittle, no matter how inane their words may seem. It's important to remember there is some truth in all things, else the thing in question literally would not exist.

Fear is what keeps you from letting go. Fear is what keeps you from attempting to understand and accept others. And it is this fear that will ultimately destroy you. I have seen this fear in many eyes, even of those who claim to be accepting. "Acceptance of others" seems to have more to do with wanting others to accept them. This is okay of course, but when it becomes so deeply engrained as to completely override one's need for self-improvement, then it becomes just a crutch, as harmful as any other.

I keep hoping for the day when *it* will finally come. I have no idea what it is, but I long for it just the same. I used to think it was my Ideal, this vision of woman who apparently only exists in my mind. Then I thought it was enlightenment, a glowing radiance signaling I was completely in tune with my Golden Orb. For the longest time I thought it was the "ultimate me", some magical collection of personal traits that combine to form the great guy I know I have the potential of becoming. Now I think it is simply peace. What I have come to understand is that none of these are possible without the initial belief. I know if I really wanted, I could achieve all of my desires with my very next breath. I could exhale as a mortal and inhale as a god. It is well within my power. To always be in want of something is to never truly appreciate what you do have. To pine for the ideal companion is to lose the companionships I do have. To always be looking for some ultimate in myself is to overlook the good that is already there.

And peace is not a place, not a city or a river bank, but a state of mind. I know this has become cliché, but it's true nonetheless. The only universe you can control is the one inside your own skin. To want anything else is not only foolish, but insane. What you will find is that when you get your innards in tune, the Universe will start singing with you, and many partners will come along to join in the chorus. Beware the sour notes and those who only want to feed off your rhythm - those who are not in tune themselves. Help them as they allow, but not to your own detriment. And know that in order to be heard you have to always be willing to sing a different note. Do not get stuck on one verse. Life is a symphony, play it for all it's worth. Believe in magic and you will be a magician. Believe in love and you will be a lover. Believe in Life and you will truly live. And *that*, my friends, is a wonderful thing.

My life is one gigantic roller coaster. Sometimes I exist on a plane that is indeed quite admirable and sometimes I plunge to depths many would have difficulty appreciating. But all in all I consider myself to be on a fairly stable and relatively elevated plane. All of my rationalizations however, do not excuse the fact that I continue to avoid inhaling my Godself. I should stand up from this very table, hover just slightly off the ground, and radiate love, peace, and joy like a beacon. I want to, I really do. I keep telling myself that someday I will. I keep saying in an emergency that is exactly what I would do. That my Godself will come forth and do whatever it is a Godself is supposed to do in such situations. The question is, can I do that now?

"Peace to all"... a quote from Aaron James

*Monday May 7th 2001*

Yesterday I was walking the road to Chapel Hill, looking down at the gravel moving along under my feet, and thinking about the karma conversation from earlier in the week. The lady was all but bragging about seeing a guru for twelve years and asked, with an accusatory inflection, "Have *you* ever seen a guru?" My response was that everyone I meet is a guru. What I realized yesterday was that not only every person, but every *thing* is a guru. Like the limbs of distant trees that helped me to understand logic. And the white oak that helped me to understand what it means to be the best me I can be. And the flock of geese that helped me to understand how our political system should function. And, in this instance, the collection of tiny pebbles that helped me to understand how all the various fragments of information over which I pass on a daily basis come together. Not only should there be something to learn from every person you encounter, but if you really keep your eyes open, you'll find something to learn from many things you encounter as well, especially in nature.

*Tuesday May 15th 2001,
my 38th birthday*

Have you ever had a life altering experience, one of those things you hear people talk about that made them realize just how short and precious life really is? Something that makes you quit your job, eat healthier, and spend more quality time with your kids? I believe we will experience in our lives precisely those things we need in order to grow in the direction we are intended. For example, I do know life is short and precious, but am constantly failing to live fully influenced by this realization. I'm always finding some comfy spot to hide and rest, thereby putting off until some imaginary point in the future the gusto with which I should be attacking today.

What if I subconsciously manifest just such a life altering experience as a swift kick in the ass to set my feet firmly on the passionate path? What if I suddenly found myself not facing a potential 40-50 years to accomplish the things I'm always telling myself I'll accomplish someday, but a matter of months? What would I do differently? I would probably ask CL to take a year off to bum around and see the country. I imagine she would do a pretty good job of feigning interest in all the mumbo I'd jumbo along the way.

The incident that sparked this entry happened while I was working on the deck for the lady I told you about May 5th. I was sitting cross-legged on the deck cutting the ends off of newly installed boards. When I went to set the Skill saw down beside me, I failed to realize the blade guard had jammed. As a result, the saw jumped off the deck and right into my lap, missing my femoral artery by a single layer of denim.

*Friday May 18th 2001 6:40 PM,*
*Hole in the Wall on Guadalupe, Austin*

I have decided that this will be the last official entry of my adventure as far as this book is concerned. The fact is I have said all I care to with this attempt and anything more would be akin to beating the proverbial dead horse. I have more input and editing, but still the end draws nigh. Part of what has brought me to this decision is the realization that I have a great deal to work on within myself. All accepting oneself BS aside, I continue to cling to a few habits that stand firmly in the way of my being who I should be, especially in terms of backing up much of what I have learned on this trip.

I have crawled far enough out of my cave to see the Light, although I have yet to develop sufficient strength to remain there. I, like the cowards I despise, also sometimes wallow in the mud and puke on the floor of the cold dark cavern of my soul. Do I want to remain in the Light? Of course. But if I waited until I were fully capable of doing so before sharing my personal beliefs, I would never share them. There are great Shamen and Yogi for that.

Jesus said, "Judge not, that ye be not judged." Ayn Rand, through her character John Galt said, "Judge and stand ready to be judged." Who is right? They both are. Strictly speaking, you have no reason to judge anyone, as your only real concern is yourself. And since there is something to learn from everyone, it only stands to reason that this would also include those you otherwise don't particularly care for. But would you not judge a crook a crook? Would you expend energy on someone so self-loathing that all they wanted was to drain your energy? I hope not. PF separates judging from discerning, in that he only judges people as required to safeguard his own well-being, which is the same thing I'm trying to say.

I find a lot of people abusing the conveniently ambiguous phrase "human nature", mostly in trying to justify or excuse our socially fabricated frailties. I put it in the same category as the religious notion of original sin. Just because we have a few weaknesses so deeply engrained in our social psyche as to seem commonplace, is no reason to accept them as normal or as anything we can't outgrow. And never use the phrase "only human" in my presence. How are we ever going to amount to anything if we're *only* human? You may have come to think of yourself as frail and weak, but that does not give you the right to condemn the rest of us.

Would you like to know just exactly when you developed your current perceptions of yourself? From birth to age six. By the time you were six years old, you already had a clear understanding of your station in life, your general intelligence, sense of self-worth, and basic personality traits. All of this was programmed into your hungry little mind during a period of your life over which you had absolutely no control.

If you were lucky enough to have had decent parents, who treated you like a human being and didn't try to cram down your throat the same frailties that were crammed down theirs, then chances are you turned out to be a pretty decent person. But many of us weren't that lucky. So what do we do? We either spend our lives wallowing in self-pity, or we reprogram ourselves, of our own choosing and by our own hand. You've heard the old question of if people can ever really change? Well, they can. For as long as you have a cognitive bone in your body, you can change. The key is to dig as deep as possible and to work on the fundamentals. It's important to remember your parents are (were) just people too, with their own strengths and weaknesses, as well as their own programmed self-perceptions.

The way I explain it is you have to rethink everything about yourself. And some simple hypnotherapy to peek into the earliest years might help too. Just be ready for your entire world to be turned upside down. The two main reasons most people avoid the process is that: A. Your life *will* be turned upside down. and  B. You will in all likelihood dig up a few things that may not be entirely laudable. Some people think if they don't face these things, they are not real. Bullshit. Air your dirty laundry, who cares. Let those sheets flap in the breeze, it's the only way they'll ever get clean. Remember, Johnny isn't a bad boy, Johnny just received some bad information.

All I can do is share the words, after that, it's up to you. You have to weigh my words, or decide they are not worth the effort. You have to choose to live, or make the same decision. For myself, I know what I must do. I know the steps I must take to reach my next level of development. What about you? If you can think of anything I've left out then please share it. If you can think of any way to reach people beyond those I am trying, I will support you 100%.

Is there anything new to consider? I know I've asked this before, but as far as this book goes, is there anything else? Man either chooses to survive or we self-destruct, it's as simple as that. All that stuff about what it means to truly live is something we all have to work out for ourselves. I've laid out most of the practical steps I see for the future. Have wielded my whammy in an attempt to beat some sense into you, or at least jar you enough to make you susceptible to receiving some sense. Have tried to empathize by telling you what a beautiful person you were at birth and are meant to be now, even if it means completely trashing your current perceptions of yourself. Have tried to stand back and let some reflected light bounce onto the page in those rare moments I was able to bask in Universal Energy. And have even gone so far as to make it as clear as possible that I am a just a man, however hoity-toity my opinion of what it means to be a (hu)man might be.

People tick and tock to their own beat, but there is a common rhythm we all share. Deep down we all crave peace, understanding, and some sense of purpose. And contrary to popular belief (even your own?), we all crave Life. Sure, we've all fallen by the wayside from time to time, but that doesn't mean we are doomed to an eternity of wallowing in the ditch.

I have one last experiment for you. First, I want you to take a moment to look as deep inside as you are able. What do you see? Is it genuine love? Is it loathing? Is it some combination of these? Of course this last is the only answer for all of us. So now the experiment part: Imagine if everyone felt the same about themselves as you feel about yourself. Are your scales tipped a little towards loathing? If you think society is in trouble now, think about what it would be like if nobody gave a damn. Do yours lean more towards love? Imagine how wonderful life would be if everyone's did.

Want to know a secret? The result of what you see is completely within your power to alter as you see fit. No one can hate you except yourself, just as no one can be strong except yourself. To this extent, *you* are the society in which you live. Society is nothing but a collection of individuals, and each and every one of us is responsible for tipping our own scales towards love. The good news is *that* is your natural way of being. Anything less is a horrific bastardization of who you were born to be. The beautiful child you were born as still lives inside you. Do whatever it takes to scrape off the layers and *find* that child.

Want to have an epiphany? Inhale your Godself. Want to save the world? Inhale your Godself. Find your Inner Child, find Christ, embrace Buddha, do anything you have to in order to develop a more positive feeling towards yourself and a healthier outlook on life. I can't say what's to come of the adventure from this point. I'm not sure if I'll wind up in Orlando or on the moon. I may make it to the Grand Canyon one of these days or I may not. Once there, I may have some new spiritual insight or I may not. But these are all miracles waiting to happen. We spend too much time waiting for miracles and lose sight of the fact that Life itself is a miracle. We all wait for that slap in the face to wake us, or that elusive level of accomplishment, or that plane of nirvana (induced or not), and let the moments slip by unnoticed. Inversely, if we focus too much on the moments, we lose sight of the big picture. Either way we are all part of the same experiment: Human life on planet earth. The how, what, and why, we may never know, but here we are just the same. And, as with all experiments, we will either succeed or fail. But unlike the billions of Life's other experiments, this time the choice is ours. Success will be of our own making, just as failure will be by our own hand. At the very least, don't simply follow the herd into a future that, in the end, no one attempted to define.

I wish I could think of something profound for my closing statement. One would like to think an adventure follows a certain crescendo to some meaningful climax. If only life were scripted as such.

In the great scheme of things there isn't much I really Know, but I do know this: That feeling of beauty and significance we all so desperately long for is, at this moment, inside each of us. And *we* are the only ones who have the power to either keep it suppressed or release it in all its glory.

*{I cannot claim this last, as my daughter transformed what had been my rather innocuous closing statement into her own poetic contribution.}*

# ☙ Epilogue ☙

*Sunday June 10th 2001*

I'm finally *at* the Kerrville Folk Festival. I've been working in Austin all this time. This is my first weekend here and the last weekend of the festival. CL flew in last week and is here with me too.

I know there is some magic combination of words to make people understand. Some caress of the soul to awaken people to the beauty of reality, some sterling knife to slice the thin veil of heaven. The problem lies in trying to discover that combination of words in written form, to be read and interpreted by a diverse group of people. Although our Universal Radiance is similar, those things that keep our respective eyes closed are unique to each of us. The things I need to hear are not the same things you need to hear. The Truths are the same, but the words that need to be said first, the words that will help you to believe, are the tricky ones.

If you are breathing, then you too can hear the nagging little voices in the back of your mind whispering these Truths. And you will keep hearing them until the day you stop breathing, but they are nothing to be afraid of. They may be contrary to nearly everything you've been led to believe about yourself, but the quiet Truths are the only ones that matter. Call it the breath of trees or the word of God, we all hear them. As such, we are all Buddha, Mohamad, and Christ.

*Thursday June 14th 2001*

One of the tricks to being on an adventure is always being ready for whatever may pop up. CL and I are on a mini road trip to Orlando and are currently sitting in the apartment of a nurse from Biloxi. There we were, happily cruising down I-10 (she was taking a nap and I had just roused myself from daydreaming about what it would be like to have an army of personal assistants), when I saw a nurse on the side of the road huddled over the right rear tire of her SUV. It took a hundred yards or so to coax Louie to the side of the road, and by the time I made it back to her she had gotten back in her truck and was laying her head on the steering wheel. Apparently she had gotten sick at work and was on her way home when she got sick again. The first thing I noticed was she was pregnant, which made me even more concerned. So we drove her to her house and are now waiting on her husband to come and take us to Louie so we can get back on the road.

We left Austin around 2:30 on Tuesday and tried to sleep in the truck Tuesday night, although it was more like being a Grand Casino buffet for the mosquitoes than sleeping. Last night we stayed in New Orleans with a good friend from Memphis who moved down last year. He's one of the few people in my life who has found the balance between not letting me spout too much BS, while valuing what I have to say in general.

Right now we're watching *Of Mice and Men* at the nurse lady's house. I wish I had the capacity of a Steinbeck (or a Malkovich) to rip open the soul of man and provide such a brilliant display.

*Saturday June 16th 2001*

Well, we made it. Barely. We got in just after midnight on Thursday, after pushing it 17 hours from New Orleans. I'm now back at CL's apartment, trying to find a job and a place of my own, or a larger place for the three of us.

I've spent the last couple of hours editing Book I, and am pretty depressed over how naive and bitter much of it sounds. It's not easy to go over journal entries from what now seems like ages ago. I liken it to being a premed student in the morgue observing your own autopsy. Who am I to think I may have stumbled onto some combination of ideas that would be of any use to anyone? Why am I pretending to pursue a life in writing when I never really gave my all to my first career of architecture? Why do I feel it necessary to imagine such drama in our future? Where are the magic pills that make it seem so easy for everyone else to just go along? Why do I feel the need to project my own weaknesses on others instead of focusing on healing myself? Why do I insist healing is necessary? Why do I insist life is meant to be joyful or that humans are anything special? How did I reach the insane conclusion that man is inherently beautiful and it is our negative programming that makes us otherwise? What harbinger of doom will foretell *my* future? Can I sleep now? I'm too tired to solve my own problems, I just want them all to go away. I want life to be a bowl of cherries. I want to chew grass and swish my tail in peace. I don't want to see the slaughter house looming in the distance. Why did you have to show it to me? I don't want to hear the voices, I don't want my fingers to move. I want life to be simple and easy like in the good old days. Remember when we used to march against our brother and fire lead balls at one another from a hundred paces? Remember when we used to trudge through our days and not think about what it was all for, except to praise god and pray for the grave? Why do we have to pretend anything is a big deal? What difference does it make anyway? Life goes on with or without us, with or without me. Is there a purpose? Who am I to know or care? What is man's fate? What is man? *Is* the balance of life fragile? Is there life after death? Is there anything on TV? Is there anything worth knowing or asking or answering? Is there any depth to which we will not sink to avoid being special? Will there ever be an end to the questions? Is all really all? Will Bush start WW-III by pissing off our allies? Will I ever print this goddamned book? How much do you have to study something before you know anything? Can't I engage in self-righteous rambling too? After all, this is just a hobby. Who cares that I'm using it as a delusional ploy for telling myself I'm doing something important. How hard can it be to lay on a couch and punch a goddamn keypad?

*Friday June 22nd 2001*

I dreamt of SJ last night, for the first time in a while. I'm still editing Book I, which refers to her quite a bit and likely explains the renewed stirrings. I remember she was so lovely and full of stories to tell me. She had been working as a lifeguard of all things. I can't remember much about the dream, but I can still see her smile. She has the most astounding way of making me feel... well, special. It seems there should be a word with more oomph to it, but special will have to do. The major debt I owe her is that she raised the bar quite extraordinarily high, which has been a good thing. No woman I've met since has come close to capturing even a fragment of my attention away from her. My real attention that is, the kind that matters.

Even the haughtiest of us tend to take love for granted sometimes, but I have a hard time accepting love as some great, inexplicable phenomenon in and of itself (i.e. something more than a heightened sense of awareness and appreciation.) I do know however, that of everything available in our emotional bag of tricks, it is love that is the most significant and love that will eventually save us. It sounds so cliché and so damned easy. But you can't love anyone until you love yourself. And in this case, one bad apple *does* spoil the whole bunch girl.

We're always hearing about society this and human nature that, but you rarely hear about the individual. No program or covenant or idea or theory will work until it is applied to the individual. It is only within your soul and my soul and the soul of your neighbor and the soul of the person you love, that the world will be saved. You have no greater task than to ensure the radiance of your own orb. Beyond this your next greatest task is to help others to illuminate their own.

*later same day*

I want to wake up tomorrow and go into my two-car, air conditioned garage and spend the day tinkering on any one of a dozen projects in progress: Architectural models, invention prototypes, paintings, you name it. Then I want to sit down at the Steinway with CL and bang out a bit-o-jazz. Then it's off to the car show where Louie walks off with multiple trophies. Then a quick jaunt to DC to answer Bush's domestic and economic policy questions. A few hours of gallery hopping in the Village, followed by the symphony in Boston. Sunday morning is fresh fruit and coffee by the pool, brunch with Jimmy Carter (who's looking to pass the torch), a book signing, a motivational speech to the Atlanta Businessmen's Association, then off to Paris for a two day summit with world leaders. Wednesday is spent at Pei's office in Manhattan planning the future of built environments. Friday it's off to LA for backup vocals on the Allman Brothers' latest album, followed by a weekend of serious partying, interspersed with a few guest appearances: Monday night on Leno, Tuesday in Chicago for Oprah, then back home to the garage, and it starts all over again.

There is no limit to the grandiosity with which I envision life, only the realities with which I deal with it. With so many people in the world it seems our ability to create such incredible realities would be magnified. I guess we can't all be Dixie Chicks, but who decides who is and who isn't?

*Wednesday June 27th 2001*

When I was in the 6th grade, my class took a field trip to one of my classmates houses. We walked down the alley from our elementary school and into her backyard. I remember they had a garden and several chickens, which seemed out of place in the heart of midtown Memphis. In high school this girl's brother and I became pretty good friends, so I hung out at their house quite a bit. By this time the backyard was an overgrown mess, full of the typical collection of lower middle class junk like tires, a boat hull, dog run, the seat out of an old van, etc. Last night I dreamt I was again walking through this backyard and into the backdoor, but this time the yard was nothing but dirt and dog shit. There were glimpses of a dog or two and a homemade doghouse, but what I remember most is seeing two or three kids playing in this filth. I remember thinking to myself, "Who would let their kids play in dirt and dog shit!?"

When I awoke this morning and remembered the dream, I was immediately struck with the analogy: Isn't that how we raise our children? We cast them into the fenced-in backyards of our limited scope of life, then expect them to play, live and grow, in the dirt and dog shit of our pathetic misperceptions of existence. So these beautiful progeny are turned into crusty heathens and we blame it not on ourselves, but on human nature. The only escape is to close their minds to this reality by any means possible. Then they grow up, squirt a few sperm into any willing vagina, and the horrific cycle starts all over again.

### *Monday July 2nd 2001*

Things aren't going so great for me in Disneyland. I've been here 2 1/2 weeks and still haven't found work. All the rest of this journey (and many times before) I landed a job at the drop of a hat. I'm not sure what's wrong here. I've already had to trade my guitar for a set of used tires. (It's okay, I can't play, it's just something that's always been on the wish list.) The other day I even wrestled with the notion of selling the laptop, but I'd just as soon lose a leg or sell Louie. CL's mother is being pretty decent about the whole thing. I mean, not many people would let an overfed, longhaired, leaping gnome sleep on their couch and eat their food without paying rent. I know I'm here mostly due to her suggestion, although I certainly didn't need much prodding. I can't imagine what it is I'm supposed to be doing differently, if that is in fact what the fate gods are trying to tell me. I don't have gas money to leave even if I wanted to.

I wonder to what extent I'm allowing myself to see the signs. Maybe there's a subconscious voice calling much louder than I realize to not abandon the adventure. I still don't feel like I've gotten any on me this trip. It's all been rather cush, however strange at times. What sort of drama would open my eyes to whatever it is I'm supposed to be seeing? I have my financial obligations to CL to think about, I say. Granted, if not for these then I would be out west somewhere at this very moment. Not that I'm complaining mind you, I'm just trying to rationalize the fact that I'm not with complete freedom to do as I please. There's nothing gnawing at my gut too heavily, I'm just wondering why things aren't falling into place.

*Wednesday July 4th 2001,*
*Happy Independence Day*

I think for a lot of people, life becomes a perpetual treadmill of devising ways of making it through the day. We get taught this early on, by waiting for the bell to ring, then for summer, then for graduation. This throws us on a path of practicing the same routine through college, then marriage, then saddling ourselves with a ton of bills, all so we won't question what it is that makes us get out of bed in the morning. Then we wait for kids, then for our kids to graduate, then for retirement, then joyfully await the grave. What the hell is that? I've wasted countless hours over the last two weeks waiting for that job offer that still hasn't come. Lying on the couch thinking how great it would be to have a garage to work on a few projects, instead of whipping out the projects right there on the living room floor. Even now all I am doing is blowing smoke, all in the comfy, sterile environment of that same coffee shop from Christmas. Even working on the book has seemed tiresome. What's going on? It could be that the banality of this place, combined with the looming responsibility of holding a steady job, are sucking my inspiration and energy. It could be that underneath the layers I've shed over the last few months lies a lazy good-for-nothing bum. It could be all I want is to scream from the mountaintops and anything less is meaningless. I've tried to console myself to the daily grind. I tell myself that it's only for two more years. Any grown man should be able to squelch his personal passions for two years, right?

But this goes against everything I call myself having learned on this adventure. Personal passion is what drives any meaningful growth. Where do my passions lie? What makes me want to get out of the bed in the morning? How guilty am I of partaking in the circus of prolonged self-deceit? What lies beyond this? I'm thinking of Charlton Heston's character in *Ten Commandments*, when he's on his last leg in the desert. The narrator says something to the effect of, "Now the steel has been purified and is ready for the sword." I've never undergone such purification. I keep telling myself I can do it slowly, over a period of years, but what this really means is I want my purification without the pain and discomfort of being on my last leg. I tell myself I could be open for such an ordeal but right now just isn't a good time. I have CL to think about, I say. What if I couldn't afford my financial obligations? What if she had to leave her expensive private school? Would this set her on the wrong path or a path more true?

I'm afraid the awful truth may be I do not believe in myself or my ideas strongly enough to risk subjecting her to my trying to find out. Her having to leave school because I failed to uphold my responsibilities could spark a chain of events that would eventually cause her to want to have nothing to do with me. I would wind up a loveless, homeless, gutter-drunk, full of bitterness for everything and everyone around me. My reality would consist of clearing a spot in the mud to lay my head, trying to find enough dry cardboard to keep warm. Begging nickels for another pint of whiskey, ignoring my stench to ever worsening degrees, quietening the voices in my head by any means necessary, and continuing to gaze upon every female who passes, wondering if she could be the one. Sharing my sad tale of being forgotten by my daughter to any unfortunate ear who would listen. Eating Salvation Army sandwiches and giving them a sheepish "Thank you", so they can go home feeling good about themselves. Digging spoiled fruit out of dumpsters, finding some way to pull yet another rotted tooth, and wondering why my body refuses to quit when my spirit refuses to go on.

I can see only two possible futures available to me. Either I will succeed in my quest for a joyful existence or I will fail miserably. I will not be able to tolerate much more lingering somewhere in the middle. Is now the time to decide? Do I dare risk it? How can I pull it off with as little collateral damage as possible? Do I condemn CL to having to make the decision to either join me or hate me? Hers is the only opinion that matters. Hers is the only life outside of my own that risks upheaval. The adventure has been relatively sedate so far. I could use some help here. I could use someone to hold up a movie screen showing my future, which way to go and how to get there. I want someone to tell me everything is going to be alright. It's like I'm five years old all over again, sitting all alone in the middle of the living room floor, crying and wondering when my mommy is coming home. But this time I don't feel so afraid... as confused.

# ෫ Book IV ෫

*Sunday July 8th 2001 8:45 PM*

Yesterday I started to write, "I'm feeling like I should try and resolve my feelings for my family", because I was feeling guilty for all the bad things I said about them in Book I, but all I managed to do was enter the date. The rest wouldn't come. Now I'm on a Greyhound bus on my way back to Memphis. I called my dad today to see if he had forwarded any mail lately and learned my middle brother, the one I've so lovingly called DAB, has been in yet another drunk driving accident. It's strange to speak of family so matter-of-factly, but my strategy to date has been to pretend their problems were not mine, that there was nothing I could do to help them.

It's hard to determine when to offer help and when to hold back. Certainly you can't help those who don't want to be helped, but who doesn't want to be helped? Most of the time we offer the wrong kind of help or for the wrong reasons. The first thing must be for the person to realize they are worthy of help, then for those of us doing the offering to ensure our primary motivation is an honest appreciation for the radiant being they are meant to be.

There are dozens of pieces to this very complicated puzzle buzzing around inside my head. Actually, I'm not going back to Memphis just because DAB is in trouble again. Although this should be reason enough, it was not the event that made me take action. It seems our oldest brother, JR, is hooked on crack cocaine. When my father told me, I had to ask him three times just to be sure it wasn't my imagination.

Obviously I felt the gravity of the situation warranted tacking on another chapter to the book.

As I was leaving, CL and her mother both asked why I felt I had to go. I said I wanted to show JR he had the power to heal himself, adding that if I could convince him, I could convince anyone. The truth is I feel this is fate ripple I've been waiting for. I've been in Orlando for more than three weeks and have not been able to find a job. The whole time I've been wondering why, from a "what is it I'm really supposed to be doing" standpoint. Now I've been given an opportunity to resolve my family relationship - for good or bad, once and for all - *and* put my money where my mouth is, all in one fell swoop.

Today on the phone I actually made my father cry. I told him the reason his sons were so messed up was because they were made to feel so worthless as children and have simply never recovered. In his defense however, he too was made to feel unwanted all his life because of being a shotgun baby. I don't hold out much hope that I can help him, he is 68 years old and very likely too far gone. But I have claimed that for as long as our biological units continue to function, our spiritual beings can recover. If our family is going to heal, it needs to start with him.

The hardest part will be convincing them to rip apart everything they think they currently believe and start from scratch. When a person is programmed from infancy to think they are worthless or unwanted, literally everything has to be rebuilt from the ground up. My father's and brothers' entire self-perceptions have always been tainted by the seed of guilt placed in their heads on day one.

Maybe I will finally get a chance to confront my father about making me feel so useless as a teenager and my mother for my deep-seeded fear of abandonment. One thing is certain, I'm not going to Memphis to pussy foot around and pretend everything is alright. I am going to rip the lid off the proverbial powder keg and resolve this thing one way or the other. Yes, I am going in on a high horse, but they will by god listen or I will walk away and never look back. This is my chance to take a stand. All the times I've spent living my life in second gear are finally about to come to a head.

But I'm predicting. I have to be careful of the old tendency to over-dramatize, but that seems almost impossible in this case. My big brother, the man who was next to Jesus and John Wayne for me as a child, is *hooked on crack fucking cocaine!* How can you over dramatize that?! That's what makes this all so real. Like the trauma I wanted without having to experience the trauma myself. I have walked away from my family before, I can do it again. I can get just deep enough into this situation to see how far they will let me, and can scoot at the drop of a hat. One thing is certain: On the other side of this situation I will either finally have a family or will once and for all be completely free.

My main reason for going home is I have to see my brother for myself, otherwise I would never truly believe it. Just as we have become immune to stories of death on the evening news, I would remain immune to my brother's plight. I've had visions of him breaking down when he sees me, his baby brother. I've also thought of convening a family meeting at our old house in North Memphis where we lived before moving to Jonesboro in 1970. It's the last place we were all together as a family, however dysfunctional. I thought maybe being together at the old place would stir up childhood memories, both good and bad, which would help set the stage for confronting the dysfunction. Most of my memories from there are fairly benign. My psychological abuse didn't kick in until we moved back to Memphis when I was 12. But the crap they try to feed us as teenagers is easier to deal with because we can at least see that coming.

## Monday July 9th 2001 6:26 AM

Good morning from Atlanta. I thought the saga could use lightening up a bit, so I opened the laptop to tell you about the trip so far. There's not much prior to now, but as the Atlanta suburbs were flickering in and out of my dreams, I was startled to full consciousness when the trainer (I guess our driver is new and still under observation) said, "Whoa dude... you were nodding off... but at least you were boogying straight ahead." Yep, nothing like a dozing bus driver to make you keep your eyes open! And then he missed our exit, not once, not twice, but three times! So this put the driver on edge and the passengers on edge, and just about the time we were finally pulling into the station, these two edges decided it was time to dance.

### 11:36 AM CST Nashville

Man, I had this great Dave Barry thing going and the laptop battery shut down without warning. As I was trying to say, the driver was having serious words with a passenger, even the supervisor chimed in. All the guy was trying to do was lodge a very logical complaint. Not only did the driver act like he was at no fault whatsoever, but he went on to say that we, "Should be grateful that (we) got to sleep while he drove." Whatever.

I haven't had any new thoughts regarding the situation, other than trying to picture the scene of seeing JR for the first time. I think I'm just going to tell him I wanted to see him one more time before he died, hopefully making the point I feel his death is imminent. I doubt things will be much different with DAB, given he's been in this mode for years. I'd like to have one big group healing, with my mom and dad included, but that's stretching the limits of hope. I've learned enough to know I cannot simply waltz in and save the day. That people - even family - are not going to genuflect before me and humbly receive my saving graces. I've also learned to avoid the pain of failure in such situations. Not failure of course, just the pain.

If I have a trick up my sleeve, it's the whole "for as long as you breathe" thing. I know every cell of JR's body craves life. I know the energy that keeps his particular collection of cells together *is* Life. The problem lies with a simple misperception of his brain, that thing between our ears we mistakenly believe is somehow greater than Universal Energy. Surely he has seen the depth of his fears and the many dark caverns of his soul. I'm hoping his steel is ready for the sword. I am hoping he has reached the breaking point.

If I had stayed in Orlando and gotten a call a month from now saying he was dead, I would have never forgiven myself for not showing I at least cared enough to try and help. What bothers me is why my nephew (who we will call OB) hasn't been able to resolve this. He is a much stronger man than I am. I guess it's because so far he's relied primarily on prayer. If prayer is going to work, it has to come from his father. For as long as JR is filled with fear and loathing, he will continue to manifest negatives in his life. Outside energy intervention pales in comparison. Besides, God didn't invent crack, why should we think God is going to save us from it?

And I've thought about my high school sweetheart too. The similarity of circumstances is almost too creepy. I would love to see her... Well, would like to see her... Well, I'm intrigued by the idea anyway.

*Wednesday July 11th 2001,*
*OB's apartment in Arkadelphia*

The Shock Stage. That's what my sister-in-law calls my current take on the crack situation. We were talking about all the stages she's gone through: Anger, disbelief, faith, and I said I just couldn't quite grasp how I felt. I do know this much however, my brother is too far gone to hold out any hope.

The one thing that didn't occur to me before was just how I would feel when I saw this man standing in front of me. I know I felt some sort of pain for a minute or two after I first got the news in Orlando. At the time, I attributed it to the portion of my brother who was important to me growing up. But sitting and talking to him, I can't say I felt much more than if I were talking to one of the street people I had befriended before leaving Memphis.

Here's another thing I've realized: I no longer feel any guilt over my decision to sever relations with my family. And for the first time in my life I can honestly say I don't feel any chips on my shoulder, nothing recognizable anyway.

The timeline of how yesterday unfolded isn't quite dramatic enough for the Hollywood ending I had imagined. I didn't get to kick down the door of a crack house and drag JR out with guns blaring. I didn't find him curled up in a corner, either trippin' or Jones'n. He hadn't shriveled up and lost all his teeth. All that happened was I went to one of his job sites and he came in about ten minutes later. He wasn't as shocked to see me as I thought he would be, especially given that 48 hours earlier I was still on my adventure, in Australia for all he knew. He just asked what I was doing in town, to which I replied, "I'm here to see how my hero is doing." The thing that blows me away is this has been going on for over four years. OB didn't find out until Christmas of '99, my dad a couple of months ago, and me on Sunday. Where were the ties that bind? Why didn't his wife sound the alarm a long time ago? Why didn't I check in more diligently?

Crack is the most insanely addictive substance you can imagine. I've never tried it, and pray I never do, but from what I understand it's even more debilitating than heroine. This is the sort of thing that no matter what balance of fear and love a user may have, it can completely derail everything from the first toke. Forget the whole notion of actively participating in human evolution, increasing social intimacy, and that "all is all" crap. This throws it all out the window. It's like replacing the blood in your veins with Clorox, like replacing your brain with a helium balloon. There is no relating to the person because the person no longer exists. The man I spoke to yesterday, the man I hugged and traded 'I love you's with, is not the man I once loved, feared, and hated. The biological entity I spoke to yesterday was a hollow shell, a wraith occupying a human body. I have no hope whatsoever for his recovery. I no longer have an oldest brother.

Why did it not pain me to type that? Am I really so cold? Or am I just so thoroughly pragmatic that I can turn off the feelings that should be there, the feelings I have decided would be pointless and wasted? I do know there remains an avenue of concern and that is for OB and the rest of his family. Given the odds in this war I have declared, I know my energies would best be spent on them. I can't afford to waste emotion on the passing of my brother.

And one thing I've learned about my "for as long as we breathe" assertion, is it is a fairly grandiose and not entirely scientifically supportable concept. I mean I still believe it, but there comes a point when a person's physio and psychological malfunctions become so entrenched that they are all but impossible to reach. My sister is also a good example of this. We were talking yesterday and I could see in every line of her face that she is firmly attached to the particular set of beliefs she feels best helps her to maintain. However she might feel about a scientific explanation of God (which came to me quite clearly last night), or the possibility that all major religions share the same basic root (even Humanism), she is firmly attached to the particular semantics she associates with Christianity. It would do no good at this point to try and supplant her belief system with something more universal. (Although supplant is too harsh a word, it would be more akin to a field of wild flowers slowly overtaking a shallow pond.) As long as it gets her through the day, any attempts to share my ideas would best be spent on someone more receptive. She is at her particular level in the ideological hierarchy and will in all likelihood remain exactly the same for the rest of her days.

Does this mean I accept defeat as regards the notions of Inner Child epiphany or inhaling your Godself? No, not in the least. It simply means I've seen concrete evidence of the barriers we place in our way. And as long as the result is not imminently detrimental to the individual in question, there are those with greater needs to focus on.

*Thursday July 12th 2001 7:32 AM*

I'm beginning to think maybe I opted out of this situation way too soon. I was relieved to hear my brother say the things he said about being on the road to recovery, but have been seriously doubting he was telling the truth. The one gift cocaine addicts have is they can say anything they think you want to hear, and usually quite convincingly. It was good to see him in relatively decent spirits. But at our celebratory lunch I could almost swear he did something in the bathroom because when he came out, his eyes were all bloodshot and his pupils were dilated. When I asked him about it, he just acted like I was ragging on him.

His wife told me he has been on the road to recovery many times over the years but failed every time. He says he doesn't like the idea of going to support groups because they, in his opinion, have nothing to offer him. Either way I hope this situation gives me the brick wall of reality I need. The wall that provides both the final separation from my past and the base from which to propel myself into the self-actuated future of my dreams.

In the end, none of the drama or self-importance or imaginary need for self-improvement or hopes and dreams or longing for love or concern for lost friends or fond memories or painful memories or delusions or expectations, amount to anything worthy of even a fraction of our time. All we can do is live the life that is before us right here and now. We can dream of a future, but the work to create it has to happen today. We can dream of a better self, but the work to bring that person to the fore has to happen in the present. I long and want and dream and crave and procrastinate and sit on my laurels and berate myself and inflate myself and accuse and assume and expect better, more than anyone else I know. But all I can do from this day forward, all I can ever do every moment of every day for the rest of my life, is to deal with the realities of that moment. Even this moment, the one right here, where I'm typing these words, has to be lived for the best it can be.

And just to pay one last homage to the habit of always dreaming of the future, let me say that I hope at some point all of our sequential moments and respective works add up to the future we deserve. None of us can afford to wallow in self-defeating mediocrity any longer. None of us can click our heals and instantly create an existence of wonder and beauty. None of us can wave a magic wand and make all the pain and suffering (and addictions) disappear. No one person holds all the answers or the right combination to the vault where Truth is contained. None of us know what it's all for, where we came from, or where we're going. But at least we can work together to help provide a better life for one another. We have to get over our blame. We have to purge our socially fabricated frailties. We have to stop thinking we can produce a magic cure-all pill and simply begin the daunting task of rebuilding every fragment of society from the ground up. If we are to survive, this is how it must be done.

*Friday July 13th 2001 7:09 AM,*
*back at JR's*

Well, I finally had the showdown I wanted. It didn't go entirely as anticipated, but now at least I can say I gave it a shot.

After yesterday's entry, OB and I left his apartment and headed for Memphis. I had spent an hour on the phone with his mother and learned JR hadn't been home for two nights, which means he'd been on a jag since the minute our wheels hit the highway Tuesday afternoon. All his grand talk about being on the road to recovery was a crock, just as I had suspected. She and I had a good talk, not only about this situation but also about life in general. I told her that her only real option was to completely cut JR loose. That all she was doing was helping him pretend he is a husband and father and semi-respectable businessman, when he's really just a crack addict. That he's sitting on the fence between his dream world of being a man and the reality of being an addict. That her only hope is to let him go, so that hopefully when he wakes up in the gutter six months from now, he will find within himself whatever it takes to want to heal.

I didn't tell OB about the jag until we were on the road. I also told him about the talk with his mother and went on to say there was a very real possibility his father may not have what it takes to want to heal when that make or break moment in the gutter comes. I can't say I was astonished when he told me he felt the same, that he had exhausted all the energy he could afford on the situation and was ready for whatever drastic measures were necessary. Having lost faith in his father's ability to recover, his primary concern was for his mother and sisters. At some point during our conversation we decided to try direct family intervention and, without my noticing when or how, detoured north towards Jonesboro.

*Saturday July 14th 2001,
back at Dad's breakfast table*

I've been thinking of adding a few sections to the book in an effort to expound upon some of the things I've been trying to say all these months. I've tried to edit as little as possible, because frankly, trying to go back and clarify my ramblings at this point would require a fairly major re-write. Hopefully your patience has gotten you this far and we can now share a few thoughts together in peace.

I think I'm finally over the "woe is me" garbagio, even though I'm currently sitting at ground zero and the chief commandant and his mistress are asleep in the next room. My mother and father and I have not slept under the same roof in almost thirty years. (Did I mention they have been seeing each other again, starting the very evening of AO's funeral?) When I walked by my dad's bedroom they were spooning like newlyweds. In their peaceful slumber they revel in the portion of their beings that crave peace and love. I have no idea why they close this off during the day but I plan to say a word or two about it before I leave. I have to take this chance to share with them a few things I've learned, in hopes they can find a kernel or two to latch onto in whatever it is I manage to say. I know at least my father listens, because the other day when we were talking to JR, he reiterated several ideas we had shared on the drive over.

I just realized the previous entry ended without my telling you about the intervention…

OB and I called his mother and learned his dad had called saying he was at one of his job sites. One of his ploys is to go off on a jag and then reappear whenever he wants, acting like there's not a thing in the world wrong. When we were about thirty minutes away, I called him on his cell and said I wanted to see him one more time before heading back to Orlando. I said I wanted to give him a copy of a book I had recently printed but had forgotten to give him before.

After we found the jobsite and were pulling into the driveway, OB asked how we were going to pull off whatever it was I supposedly had in mind of doing. I knew no amount of dramatizing or role playing was going to work. The plan was to somehow get him in the truck and drive him home, then have as many of the family as we could gather, confront him in a round robin "you're killing yourself and your family", in-your-face confrontation. All we did was stroll in the house, ask him if we could have a minute, and stroll right back out. Luckily he followed. As he came out the front door, OB and I were closing his tool boxes and clearing out the front seat of his truck. In just as grown-up and responsible a manner as you can imagine, he said, "Do you mind if I ask what you think you're doing?" To which I responded, "Taking you home."

"I'm not going anywhere. I have a job to do and I've got to get back to it."

"If I had some crack you would leave to smoke it."

At this point we were standing on opposite sides of the driver's side door, glaring at one another through the open window, both gripping the frame, with our faces inches apart. Looking back it all seems wrought with senseless machismo, but I knew he would respond to little else. Remember, he is a scared little boy who tries to hide under a rough exterior. He is such a big man that almost everyone his entire life has fallen for this trick, but the little boy is still there. The rough hide needed bursting and I knew the little boy was on my side.

After a few such exchanges he turned to go back in the house. I had tried to implore him to get in the truck and go home, but to him it would have been ludicrous to obey the demands of his baby brother. Almost to the door, with me still ranting, he turned and said, "Well then I guess you'll just have to shoot me." This was a fairly ironic use of cliché on his part, because that's when I reached into OB's car and got his pistol from the passenger side floorboard. It was one of those bull hunter things, a semi-automatic large bore that holds 8-10 rounds, which was loaded with hollow points and had an extra clip in the holster. As insane as the prospect may have seemed, this would have put him down with one shot. What you have to realize is I was not dealing with my brother who happened to be hooked on crack, I was dealing with a crack addict who at one time happened to be my brother. I knew most of what filled his head, even in the midst of a potentially violent showdown with his own brother and son, was, "How can I get out of this so I can sneak off and get some more crack?"

He was only a step or two outside the front door and I was standing ten feet away facing him on the walk leading to the stoop. We were both aware of the fact that if he had made it in the house, getting him back to the truck would have been all but impossible. I was holding the pistol in my left hand, still holstered but unsnapped, and shoving my right index finger at him like a lance that could come flying off at any moment and pierce his skull.

And then I unleashed on him.

I'd only had occasion to use this voice once before. It's like you completely open your throat and your vocal chords become this saucer sized amplifier that every molecule of air in your lungs has to pass through on its way out. Every muscle of your torso has forgotten the actions required to inhale and only knows how to force air out the throat and at the victim. I knew if there were any fragment of a human inside the shell I was addressing, it would take a hell of a lot of convincing to reach him.

For some reason, and lucky for me, he did not respond in kind. There was no anger on his part and he made no attempt to either retreat or attack. What he did do however, was put his chin in his palm and stand there with his head lowered as if he were trying to think of something brotherly to say. Something that would once again fool me into thinking he had the situation under control. But every time he tried to open his mouth, I instantly fired back, "Shut the fuck up!" I said I knew he was just trying to think of some clever way to get out of this. Then it occurred to me his client was standing right inside and could hear every word, so I specifically used the term "crack addict". I told him not to pretend I was addressing a man or even my brother, because I knew there no longer existed inside the shell standing in front of me a man worthy of being treated with respect and understanding. That I knew every word out of his mouth would be a lie and to just shut the F up and get in the GD truck. I know at one point I made it clear I no longer had any concern for the wad of flesh I was speaking to, that my only concern was for "one of the finest men I've ever known" (my nephew), and that I would kill for him or die trying. My legs were shaking like wildfire the entire time and my left knee even started to buckle at one point. I never thought about the final act of putting a bullet in his gut, I just stood there and let the reality of the moment dictate my actions.

Would I have fired if he attacked? Would I have even been able to draw? I have no idea, and luckily did not need to find out.

I didn't notice a break in his demeanor or a spark in his face that indicated I had made my point, he just started moving towards his truck. At first I thought he was coming at me and I made one of those "what th'ell" sort of half jerks away and half jerks towards the gun. All he did was ask that we tell his boy inside to put up the tools when he was done and go home. He also asked OB to apologize to his client for my behavior. "Not for what he said, because it was all true, but for how he said it."

As we were leaving, we thought we saw his wife's van just down the road. He made one more attempt at pulling the tough hide routine and told me if I talked to her like I talked to him he would break my neck. I don't know where it came from because I was still in non-rehearsed mode, but I very calmly and matter-of-factly told him to just shut up. To my astonishment he didn't say another word the entire drive. Of course inside his fragile mind he was beyond worrying about me and more focused on how he was going to once again fool his wife. When we got to his house I asked him to wait outside. I wanted the intervention to begin immediately and knew it would be a lot safer if we were all away from the temptation of knives or other weapons. He of course completely ignored me, and on his way in the back door he said to me over his shoulder, "Now *this* would be a good place to die." Still in pseudo-machismo mode I said, "Yes it would."

The next thirty minutes or so were spent with him talking to his wife in private. I knew she was on her last leg with him and we had already talked about how he would try to say anything to fool her. Then he went upstairs to take a shower. When he came down he was wearing a 4" folding Buck knife on his belt. There was one moment when he was bending over to tie his boots that I tried to sneak it out of the sheath, but he felt it and instantly grabbed my hand. I said his wearing a knife made me nervous and asked if he would he please put it in a drawer, which he did with little argument. When he was dressed, he took his dinner plate and went outside to eat. A few minutes later our dad and DAB drove up. At first our dad was all "Hello!" and "How they hangin?" like nothing was wrong, until I went right up to him and asked him to please focus.

The rest of the story will have to wait for now. The folks are awake and it's time for round two. Time to pray for the right words and willing ears. Time to hope that for once I can relate to these people as human beings, both from my own perspective and theirs. Time to finally try and say all the things I've complained to you about for so long. Time to brush the chips off my shoulder, without even bothering to examine the shattered remnants as they crash on the floor.

*Wednesday July 18th 2001,*
*back in Orlando*

So many things have happened since the last entry that it's difficult to know where to begin. Even the events of today are important. I'll just start by recounting the actual intervention, then the anticipated round two from above.

As I said before, we were able to get JR outside, with myself, nephew, dad, DAB, and sister-in-law. There's no real script to replay, only a few key highlights that seem important. At first JR tried to pull the whole "I know I've screwed up but I've seen the light and can get better" routine again. He was brutally honest about some of the things he had done and how he had managed to get away with them. He said during the time since OB and I had left 36 hours earlier, he had smoked $500 worth of crack. Part of the problem is his addiction remains a secret and most of his friends still see him as a church going husband and father. Even his clients give him cash advances, much of which he somehow manages to parlay into crack. He even told us he had hocked his plumbing tools the day before.

You can imagine much of the rest: "You've really let us down" and "We've heard it all before". I threw in a "Useless piece of crap", mainly because it felt good to release the anger. We talked about several options of trying to keep him clean, including our dad or his wife going to work with him every day. We felt he stood a better chance of staying away from the stuff if he were given no opportunities to sneak off by himself, which being self-employed offers plenty of. For some reason my ideas of telling his church or putting a tell-all half page ad in the paper both got shot down.

Then the intervention took an odd turn. DAB, who had been mostly quiet to that point, decided it was time to put in his two cents worth. At first he was very genuine in trying to explain to the rest of us what it was like to smoke crack (something he said he had tried), but this quickly gave way to his acting like the intervention was just a crock - all the while with a mixed drink in his hand. Then he got on the old kick of trying to make me look like a meddling pansy know-it-all. I can't figure out why it matters to me now, but looking back I realize this is when I should have let the intervention evolve to include him too. At the time I told myself the focus shouldn't switch to him, that this would only take away from JR. But now I see this was when the pressure cooker was really ready to blow. Under the circumstances, maybe a good old fashioned family brawl would have been just the ticket. But they are both monsters, my nephew was armed, and my sister-in-law was already at her wit's end. Besides, some things just don't matter, you know? DAB is a drunk alcoholic and although I know why (he even gave those precise reasons during his rant), he refuses to drop his tough façade and let us help. Part of me knows for a GD fact that deep down he wanted to be challenged, that he was ready to break, but part of me was (and still is) bored with the whole prospect. We were there for JR, and while their problems are related in root cause, and attacking both would have helped to expose that root, it was all too much to take at the time. We were managing a somewhat civil discussion regarding a serious family situation and that was enough to deal with.

All in all, I'm not sure the talk did any good. A few of the things that needed to be said were said, and a few of the ideas that needed to be shared were shared, but I can't say if any of it helped. After my dad and DAB left, JR and his family continued to talk outside for a few more minutes. Then JR went upstairs and slept for the rest of the day and night. My sister-in-law and I had another excellent conversation about life and joy and the importance of inner passion. She has always been a Christian, so I never thought she would take any of my Humanist BS seriously. She agreed the bulk of my brother's problems stemmed from the fact that he was beaten as a child and, as such, never connected with the beautiful little boy he was meant to be. I have no idea how JR and DAB feel on the inside, or what sort of nightmares they must have, but I do know they lack a fundamental aspect of what it means to be human, namely a deep-seeded craving for peace. Maybe the little boys are still in there, but if they are, it would take a lot more work than I'm willing to muster to find them.

I spent that night at JR's, then they dropped me off in Memphis on their way to a job in middle Tennessee. I slept most of that day until my dad got home from work. Then I picked up my mother and the three of us spent some time going through old family photos. It was an okay time, I guess. With some of the things that had been said during the week, my feelings for my father had matured quite a bit, although I was still uncomfortable around my mother. The next morning (Saturday) was when I told you about the standoff and the much anticipated airing of parental woes.

## Thursday

"Mother Detachment Syndrome"

I typed that phrase while sitting at the breakfast table with my mother last Saturday. It's the term she says is used to describe what's wrong with her. She was a victim of the Tennessee Children's Home Society black market baby scandal perpetrated by Georgia Tann in Memphis during the 30's and 40's. The story, as I understand it, is her parents were too poor to keep her when she was born so they left her at the children's home saying they would return for her in a year, presumably when their situation improved. What they didn't know was they had left their child at what amounted to little more than a baby factory. (There is a movie about the scandal called *Stolen Babies* starring Mary Tyler Moore and Lea Thompson.) Because my mother had a wandering eye, which made her undesirable fodder for the mill, she was all but abandoned in her crib for the first year of her life. By the time her parents returned however, she had been adopted by my sainted grandmother. I have to believe my mother received a great deal of love in her new home and certainly a more promising future than her birth home could have provided. The problem is her very earliest conditioning was completely devoid of any love or nurturing whatsoever.

It wasn't until my mother was well into her third marriage, when she would have been in her early-to-mid fifties, that I started to notice a serious decline. Although we never spent much time together, I began to notice that when she watched TV she would drift off as if she were in a drug induced stupor. Then all attempts at personal hygiene or keeping a clean house began to completely disappear. By the mid 90's, if I were to see her out somewhere in a store, I would zip to the next isle before she could see me. I was too ashamed to be reminded that this haggard old wretch was my mother. Whenever I would go to visit my grandmother (who lived next door), I would try to sneak over so she wouldn't see me. Every time she did, she would come over and completely derail any hopes of decent conversation by rehashing meaningless crap from my childhood. My mother was the nucleus around which all the loathing I felt for my family was centered. It was not until the moment we sat down to talk last Saturday that I ever imagined I could possibly feel any differently.

Before my dad and I had left for Jonesboro on that first trip to see my brother, I stopped by to get her take on the situation. As expected, she acted traumatized and concerned, although I have long held that people who are riddled with self-loathing are secretly thrilled by such drama. They hate themselves so much that it excites them to see others in pain and suffering. Instead of acting for their own salvation, they attempt to fill the void with an all-consuming lust for the destruction of others. This is the very essence of everything that threatens humanity. Nevertheless, I told her I was on my way to see JR and needed for her to try and understand her role in any potential healing process. I took her hands and showed her that in one was a passionate desire to live and in the other was the slow, torturous death of her existence. I asked her to think about which hand she chose, adding that the key to resolving the crisis depended on her decision.

Do you remember back in Book III, where we talked about will and intent? I believe the energies radiated by a person not only affect their own lives but also the lives of those around them, especially those to whom they are intimately connected. My mother has become such a strong source of negative energy that she is literally sucking the life out of everyone around her, thereby exacerbating her sons' respective inabilities to recover. I know my sensing this force on my own life, combined with similar vibes from my dad and DAB, was one of the biggest reasons why I had to leave Memphis.

So there I was, sitting across the breakfast table from the person who, prior to that moment, I often referred to as "the woman who bore me." But this was the long awaited round two, right? I had to give it a shot. I took a deep breath and asked her to please just listen to what I had to say. For some reason she said she would feel more comfortable if we held hands, so I obliged. The first thing I did was reiterate the necessity of choice shared earlier in the week. Actually, the *first* thing I did was read to both her and my dad the account of how OB and I managed to get JR in the truck, then my dad went off to weed-eat the front yard. I guess he felt he and I had already engaged in enough probing family banter and he wanted my mother and I to have the same opportunity.

Life, the energy that animates our biological units, is not a matter of choice, but the extent to which we *live* life is. We did not choose to be born, we did not choose our families, and we did not choose the primary circumstances of our existence. Some say these are choices made in heaven or that these things happen for a reason (like to settle the score of past lives), but this simply is not true. The only *reason* for this life, outside of the primary forces of evolution itself, is that which we choose to give it.

But because humans evolved a certain level of intelligence, which unfortunately also renders us psychologically malleable, there are far greater issues at stake for us than exist anywhere else in the animal kingdom. We seem driven by a constant need to create, or otherwise imagine, a completely unnecessary degree of drama in our lives. If it's good drama, we imagine we are happy. If it's bad drama, we imagine we are distraught. If it's mediocre drama, we imagine we are bored.

What we fail to realize (or refuse to acknowledge) is that most of this drama is manifested by our own subconscious will and intent.

The point I tried to make to my mother was that she could only help with this situation if she made the conscious decision to choose to live. That the negative circumstances of her life were a direct result of her wallowing in her hovel all day, trying to pretend the outside world did not exist. That the only way the circumstances of her life were going to improve was if she made a conscious effort to improve them. That she could not escape the past by pretending it never happened. That inside the brute hulk of a crack addict that was once her son, was the screaming remnant of a little boy who still needed her love, and that it was not too late to give it to him.

I tried to assure her I was alright, that whatever petty little problems I had to work out paled in comparison to the daunting task she faced. I wanted her to both have one less son to worry about and a potential confidant if she needed one. She seemed to get the gist of our talk and vowed to try and do better. She agreed to work harder to gain control of her own existence. Although I can't say my feelings for her have done a 180, at least I can acknowledge the potential for a renewed relationship. Only time will tell if she gains any ground. Part of me feels I should wish her luck, but part of me knows this would be falsely amplifying my concern. I want to see her recover, but more as a fellow human, as one who does not deserve to suffer, than as my mother.

You're probably wondering, as I have yet to tell you, when I began to realize that my feelings for my father were maturing. The first inkling was when he starting crying on the phone after telling me about JR. The second was when he bought me a bus ticket home. He had never before treated me like someone who might just have something to say.

On our way to Jonesboro he was very receptive to the theory of human potential and of the long-lasting impact a person's childhood has on their lives. I told him if JR had any hope of recovery, then he too would have to help reach and repair the little boy. When I said he would have to share in the responsibility of the mistreatment of his children, he became physically nauseous to the point of throwing up in the cab of the truck. That's when I knew there was hope. For as long as he maintains an emotional connection to his own little boy, even if it took the trauma of this situation to help him discover it, he stands a good chance of finding his way. And the first steps along this path are to get over his own guilt of being conceived out of wedlock and to reprogram the feelings of uselessness that were crammed down his own throat as a child. Seeing him begin to understand this is what caused me to finally overcome my lingering misgivings of him.

*later same evening*

I want to try and share the notion of God I had the other night, which is not to be confused with anything having to do with religion.

I believe that everything is energy, both the infinitesimal elements of an atom, as well as that which maintains their relative orbit. If this is so, then it also holds that what we perceive as *space* between what we perceive as *objects*, is energy as well. So now we're dealing with nothing but varying frequencies of energy, which we have chosen to perceive as ourselves and a collection of objects outside of ourselves. Now extend this concept to include those objects outside of Earth, and even the space between them, and you begin to get some idea as to the amount of energy we're talking about. Nothing exists in the Universe but energy. And if you were to take all this energy and try to imagine it in its entirety, the result would be God.

By attempting to remove ourselves from the vast pool of energy that is the Universe, we are compelled to label everything we see as outside of ourselves. That which we have imagined to be the moving force behind the myriad of events in our lives, we at some point chose to label as god. But in doing so, we only belittle the very notion of God. By thinking God is only concerned with ourselves, we establish in our minds a convenient level of importance that only skews our perceptions of everything else. Does this mean we are not important? Does this mean we are not creations of God, from an evolutionary standpoint? No, it does not. It means that the magnitude of what our various religions have been trying to tell us is much more profound than we imagined. God is not the *creator* of all things, God *IS* all things.

### Sunday July 22nd 2001

I can sense a significant change has taken place in me over the last two weeks, some final psychological hurdle that had to be cleared. Somehow the combination of events and realizations has caused me to reach a new level of comfort with myself. I first began to feel it on the bus ride to Memphis, then more so on the drive over with my dad. By the time I had reached OB's I was fairly certain of it. Now that the ordeal is behind me, I know it. It's like I had been looking in a mirror trying to see my own face since taking my first steps on this path of self-discovery eight years ago. The image had gotten clearer with each step, but even as recently as Springfield, I was amazed at how much it resembled DAB instead of me, or the me I wanted to be there.

I know there have been times I've chosen to ignore the mirror and coast on the memory of recent accomplishments or wallow in self-glory. I convinced myself that for as long as I was on a path I could overlook the occasional slip in the mud. I tried to pretend that by simply understanding how our actions impact humanity and our thought energies radiate to affect the world around us, I was somehow immune to these laws. That I was not really part of the world I was attempting to perceive and describe. That to me, life was something that happened everywhere else, but in here I was safe. That as long as my thoughts and intentions were relatively pure most of the time, my life would generally be okay and I could work to make up the rest. I never assumed I was above the laws of cause and effect, the karmic laws of the Universe, I just always felt I could handle it.

Have I grown as a person in the last 38 years? Has a significant portion of this growth occurred in the last eight? On this adventure? The answer to all of these is yes. The only difference is now I can more clearly see the man in the mirror and more adamantly refuse to turn away. It is only by pretending the mirror doesn't exist that we think we can get away with our indiscretions. Have I slipped? Yes. Will I slip again? Of course. But gone is the old double edged sword of self-berating and self-excusing.

> "I ask the Universal Energy to bring into my life the rewards of my good deeds and the punishment of my wrongs. I will neither laugh off one nor buckle under the other. I am my own man, responsible for my own thoughts and actions. I will stand proud to accept the rewards and I will stand proud to take the punishment. I know the face in the mirror is astonishingly beautiful. I will smile in amazement at its reflection, and together will remind one another of the wonder of this existence and of the joy of this life."
>
> Aaron James

All I can do is pray that someday my mother and father, brothers and sister, and all those scurrying around on the planet, will eventually be able to do the same. Life is precious people, and so are we.

PF once shared the following parable:

*One day God came to one of God's devotees and said, "Mr. Getz, you've been a loyal servant all your life and I want to reward your efforts by granting you three wishes." Stan thought about it for a minute and said, "Great man! Tell you what, I've spent the last ten years wanting to be free of my wife, I wish for a no strings divorce." Although God was shocked, God obliged. A few weeks later God checked back in and said, "Time for wish two, what do you want?" "Well God", said Stan, "I miss my wife and wish for her back." Poof, there she was, with no memory of the divorce. Then God said, "Stan, you realize you only have one wish left. If I were you, I'd think this one over and make it count."*

*After God left, Stan struggled to come up with the best wish he could think of. He even talked it over with his friends. "What if I wished for all the money I could ever use?" His friend replied, "But what about health? You could be rich but without the physical capacity to enjoy it." Stan thought about that. "Okay, then I'll wish to always have good health." "Oh great", said his friend, "Now you've got good health but you could be living in squalor, without a dime to enjoy anything." "Wonderful, now what am I supposed to do?"*

*When God came by a month or so later, God asked Stan what he'd come up with. He confessed his dilemma and asked for God's help. God admired Stan's honest attempt at making a wise decision and said, "Okay Stan, I will share with you what I would wish for if I were you. And if you think about it, it's the only logical choice. Wish for true, deep-seeded happiness, no matter what." Stan was amazed, and thus spent the remainder of his days a happy man, even in the face of the very things he thought had made him unhappy before.*

The day after I got back to Orlando, I had two interviews and got offers from both. Thursday I started working temp at one while I try to figure out my next move. Finishing this book remains a priority, as does giving Louie the complete overhaul he deserves. I know I love my daughter and remain excited about being here with her. I'm not looking forward to calling home to check on the status of my brothers, but know I have to. I continue to want many of the things I've always wanted, and the millions of crazy ideas that constantly rattle around inside my head are still rattling. I know I still crave growth, both for myself and my fellow man. But above all, I know I'm happy. And brother, you can't ask for much more than that.

# ⋳ Book V ⋳

*Friday September 14 2001 5:20 AM*

In light of recent events, I felt it was necessary to add yet another new chapter to the book.

News agencies, even CNN, continue to speak of "exclusive photos" as if the attacks were staged for the benefit of their ratings. And I continue to see interviewers prod witnesses and family members for gruesome details, including accounts of seeing people jump from the buildings and the inevitable references to "body parts." Even if you can understand how these practices may have evolved in the past, ask yourself what good can they possibly do us now?

There are millions of thoughts racing through my head at the moment, not the least of which are of CL. For the last day or so I've been wrestling with the idea of going to New York. I've called both the local Red Cross and a hotline in NYC for those who wish to volunteer professional services, but have yet to be summoned. Obviously I've been struck with the significance of these events as they relate to the premise of this book. I've never considered myself a prophet and can't honestly say the complete destruction of the World Trade Center complex is something I had foreseen. When I speak of death mongers, I mean those people walking the streets every day. Those whose every action is geared towards deceiving themselves into believing that their subconscious will and intent is not fueled by fear and loathing. And unfortunately this includes many of the people who are now in a position to aggravate this already volatile situation, including those in the media and in Washington.

*Sunday September 16th 2001*

The following is an observation by an Afghani-American writer, forwarded to me via email:

*I've been hearing a lot of talk about "bombing Afghanistan back to the Stone Age." One radio talk show host said that this would mean killing innocent people, people who had nothing to do with this atrocity, but went on to say, "We're at war, we have to accept collateral damage. What else can we do?" Minutes later I heard a TV news commentator discussing "... whether we have the belly to do what must be done." I thought about the issues being raised especially hard, because I am from Afghanistan. And even though I've lived here for 35 years, I've never lost track of what's going on there. So I want to tell anyone who will listen how it all looks from where I'm standing.*

*I speak as one who hates the Taliban and Osama bin Laden. There is no doubt in my mind that these people were responsible for the atrocities in New York, Washington and Pennsylvania. I agree that something must be done to stop these monsters. But the Taliban and Ben Laden are not Afghanistan, they are not even the government of Afghanistan. The Taliban are a cult of ignorant psychotics who took over Afghanistan in 1997. bin Laden is a political criminal with a plan. When you think Taliban, think Nazis. When you think bin Laden, think Hitler. And when you think "the people of Afghanistan", think "the Jews in the concentration camps." It's not only that the Afghan people had nothing to do with this atrocity, they were the first victims of the perpetrators. They would rejoice if someone would come in there, take out the Taliban, and clear out the rat's nest of international thugs holed-up in their country. Some ask, "Why don't the Afghans rise up and overthrow the Taliban?" The answer is: they're starved, exhausted, hurt, incapacitated and suffering.*

*A few years ago, the United Nations estimated there are 500,000 disabled orphans in Afghanistan - a country with no economy and no food. There are millions of widows, and the*

*Taliban has been burying them alive in mass graves. The ground is littered with land mines, and the farms were all destroyed by the Soviets. These are a few of the reasons why the Afghan people have not overthrown the Taliban.*

*We come now to the question of bombing Afghanistan back to the Stone Age. The trouble is, that's already been done. The Soviets took care of that. Make the Afghans suffer? They're already suffering. Level their houses? Done. Turn their schools into piles of rubble? Done. Eradicate their hospitals? Done. Destroy their infrastructure, cut them off from medicine and health care? Too late, someone already did all that. New bombs would only stir the rubble of earlier bombs. Would they at least get the Taliban? Not likely. In today's Afghanistan, only the Taliban eat, only the Taliban have the means to move around. They would slip away and hide. Maybe the bombs would get some of those disabled orphans, they don't move too fast, they don't even have wheelchairs. But flying over Kabul and dropping bombs wouldn't really be a strike against the criminals who did this horrific thing. Actually, it would only be advancing the cause of the Taliban - by raping once again the people they've been raping all this time. So what else is there? What can be done?*

*Let me now speak with true fear and trembling. The only way to get bin Laden is to go in there with ground troops. When people speak of "having the belly to do what needs to be done", they're mainly thinking in terms of having the belly to kill as many as needed, of having the belly to overcome any moral qualms about killing innocent people. Let's pull our heads out of the proverbial sand. What's actually on the table is Americans dieing. And not just because some Americans would die fighting their way through Afghanistan to bin Laden's hideout. It's much bigger than that folks. Because to get any troops into Afghanistan, we'd have to go through Pakistan. Would they let us? Not likely. The conquest of Pakistan would have to come first. Will other Muslim nations just stand by? You see where I'm going: we're flirting with a World War between Islam and the West. And guess what, that's bin*

*Laden's program. That's exactly what he wants. That's why he did this. Read his speeches and statements. It's all right there. He really believes Islam would beat the West. It might seem ridiculous, but he figures if he can polarize the world into Islam and the West, he's got a billion soldiers. If the West wreaks a holocaust in those lands, that's a billion people with nothing left to lose. That's even better from bin Laden's point of view. He's probably wrong, in the end the West would win, whatever that would mean, but the war would last for years and millions would die, not just theirs but ours. Who has the belly for that? bin Laden does. Does anyone else?*

*Signed,*
*TA*

I would like to thank TA for these words. I had been searching for an intelligent perspective on this issue and am grateful to the friend who forwarded the email. I would like to add a few concerns of my own regarding the lives of the innocent on our own soil.

I've been watching the news almost non-stop since first getting word of the attacks and have heard only limited reference to the very real dangers we potentially face here at home. It is insanely naïve to assume these attacks, as fierce and debilitating as they were, are the worst our enemies have to throw at us. We talk of sending troops to some foreign land and those of us who will remain snug in our beds give a great sigh of relief. As grieved as we certainly all are over the deaths of our fellow citizens, most of us have no idea what the horrors of war are like from the inside. But let me assure you we will get our chance. We must understand that a high-jacked airliner employed as a missile is but only one weapon available to those who wish us harm.

These words are not intended to elicit unwarranted fear, but we must not ignore the ominous future that looms before us. Many voices in the past, from the Book of Revelations to

Nostradamus, have spoken of the end of the world, the destruction of mankind, of Armageddon. Over the past century we experienced two global conflicts that many acknowledge were merely the staging ground for these predictions. With our bombing of Hiroshima and Nagasaki, we witnessed firsthand just how possible large scale destruction actually is.

Let me emphatically state that I do not believe in the power of prediction to dictate ultimate fate. I do however believe in the power of sensitive insight. We must not use these predictions as a calling into the dark void of death, but as a plea for the sanctity of Life. Predictions be damned. It is *we* who hold the reins of our fate. It is we who will act towards our own destruction or salvation. As righteous as we may feel in our quest for vengeance, now is the time to act most diligently with calm and reason. If we go into this conflict half-cocked, we will be sealing our fate as surely as the most devastating predictions have foretold.

In school we are taught of great figures from our past, of George Washington, Harriet Tubman, and Abraham Lincoln. The mere mortals among us wonder how such greatness was achieved and can't imagine ourselves in their position. What we fail to realize is that these were relatively normal people who rose to face extraordinarily abnormal challenges. Would they have preferred the normalcy of a peaceful existence and stable life? Certainly. But the one thing that separates our heroes from the rest of us is their realization that normalcy often requires suffering the abnormal. And that no one was going to step up to the plate but themselves.

Now is the dawning of a new era for humanity. We face this conflict not as a nation, or even a body of people who hold to one particular set of beliefs, but as a species faced with the possibility of its own annihilation. If you do not wish for the those most dire predictions to come to pass, if you desperately cling to the sanctity of Life, now is the time to make your voice heard. Now is the time to step up to the plate, to embrace the hero within. Tell everyone you see that you want to live! Yes we demand justice, but at what cost? Act and act decisively, but not recklessly. Fight the righteous fight, but do not injudiciously repeat past mistakes. And do not assume we are somehow immune to defeat.

Our greatest adversaries are not those who overtly wish us harm, but ourselves. Our greatest threat is not bombs or biological agents, but our own apathy. The following came to me sometime in early '96, but speaks directly to this concern:

## A Plea for Sanity

It is rumored that evil is all around us.

By some horrifying miscarriage of reason,
It is believed that if the evil is left unidentified,
Or is dispassionately referred to in the third person,
It will somehow vanish
Or leastwise not affect yourself.
For the moment, the urgency of entertainment
Plays the handy role of dissuading your recognition.

For today you can swill one more drink or indulge one more folly,
Or cower in your bed in the pretense of comfort,
And postpone awareness for just a while more.

And when someone in your village is robbed,
You whisper to your neighbor, "Thank god it wasn't one of us."
And when your neighbor is beaten,
You whisper to yourself, "Thank god it wasn't me."
And when thieves break into your home and steal your kettle,
You say, "At least they didn't steal the pot."

And when your time has come,
After thieves have stolen your property,

Burned your home and murdered your children,
Then, as you cower in a blind stupor,
As the final blows are delivered upon your head,
You realize what you should have known long ago:

That the only way to survive is to act,
That evil is impotent without your consent,
That the expanse of evil is equal to your refusal to see it,
That no task is more vital than protecting your personal welfare,
And that no one can save you but yourself.

And as you gasp your last breath,
The final flickers in your feeble mind,
Will be the regret that you failed to realize until that very moment,
That life truly is a precious gift,
And that of all these, the most precious was your own.

༄

May whomever you choose to acknowledge as a higher power, be it God or Allah, the Divine Spirit or Universal Energy, be with us all. And may the methodic, determined wisdom of the Gods be with our political leaders.

*Friday September 21st 2001*

An email to MSNBC.com:

"I only recently logged onto your site after hearing it promoted by Brian Williams. I was intrigued by the promise of such a wealth of news and information. However, as it seems with most things these days, I was ultimately disappointed after being immediately bombarded by advertisements. Isn't it enough that you have the ability to deliver much needed information without flashing casino banners smack in the middle of your home page? I understand the need for revenue, but do you have to be so blatant about it?

One of the most pervasive problems with our modern American society is that we have twisted the concept of Capitalism to mean "profits at all cost". Profits are in fact a secondary benefit of doing what our passions drive us to do. When we turn this around and put profit before passion, we are doomed to follow the herd into any pit with a dollar. We have morphed the bottom line from "how well was my soul rewarded by my actions" to "how well was my wallet rewarded by my actions". It is clear where the soul of MSNBC.com lies. In times of trial by fire, when the chaff is separated by the wind, it is only those with a healthy soul who will survive, and all the profits in the world won't change that.

I realize the issue of banner ads on your home page may seem trivial, but it speaks volumes of our current state. If any good is to come from our recent tragedies, it should be a wakeup call to heed our soul. For it is the soul of America that transcends borders and atrocity, and the soul of America that will see us through these trying times. The soul of America is an ideal, a vision, not the mere physical manifestations so easily destroyed by our enemies.

MSNBC.com is simply one masthead of a vast news empire. A tremendous percentage of our population gets its information via this empire. What kind of a message are you sending to those who so desperately need this information, when you attempt to take advantage of this need by slipping an advertisement right under the headline photo of our President?"

I'm sure mine was not the only complaint, but within a few days they noticeably toned down the banner ads.

## Saturday September 22nd 2001

Yesterday morning I sat straight up in bed and immediately began sketching a skyscraper design the gnomes had whispered into my ear during the night. I was so shocked by what I saw that I decided to apply for copyright protection, which was in the mail by noon. This is the letter I wrote to accompany the application.

"This design was created for the express purpose of rebuilding at the World Trade Center site. I chose a height of 2,100 feet because I felt it was important to rebuild with a skyscraper that surpasses anything in existence, as well as to acknowledge the promise of the 21st century.

The key to the design is the cast-in-place concrete rigid-frame, which allows for the tremendous height and durability of the structure. The frame also divides the tower into four distinct sections, joined by the juxtaposition, or 'pinwheel', of their counterparts. The strength of this feature is further enhanced by the frames engaging at each respective center point, thereby transforming what would typically be the weakest point of the frame, into the strongest. Finally, the pinwheel arrangement creates an interior safety core for isolated egress.

The basic foot print of the tower is 450' square, with the interior egress core being 150' square. The ground floor is a 50' high, 202,500 s.f. Grand Lobby. The lower tier of 51 floors are 150,000 s.f. each, with the middle tier of 36 floors being 80,000 s.f. each. The top tier of 36 floors are 50' wide beltways around the interior core of 40,000 s.f. each, and are intended primarily for residential use. This totals 12,172,500 s.f. of usable space (not including interior core) on 124 floors.

The pinwheel frame not only provides required rigidity, but also acts as fire separation between the individual sections, which means that any one vertical section could sustain damage and the others would remain unaffected. This allows ample opportunity for the inhabitants of the affected section to seek shelter or egress in the unaffected sections, which finally resolves the century old dilemma of getting inhabitants to safety during an emergency in a skyscraper, as horizontal egress is infinitely more practical than vertical.

The reason for the collapse of the twin towers was the fact that, regardless of design superiority, each building was composed of one simple vertical structure. When this structure suffered a horizontal sever, there was no chance of anything but failure. Another feature of this design that plays a dual role in terms of both durability and safety, is the structure of the tower sections themselves. The floor loading is broken into 50 foot grids, both vertically and horizontally. While this primary structure is relatively lightweight, the intermediate floors (three per grid), are even lighter. This is only possible because the vertical load bearing members do not have to be sized as required to also displace lateral load, as this is accomplished through the pinwheel rigid frame."

I realize that to most the above is just a bunch of architectural techno-speak. To put it in layman's terms, no skyscraper as yet constructed is anything more than one floor stacked on top of another. No one has bothered to resolve the two main concerns of such designs, which are how to get people in the upper floors to safety in an emergency and how to keep the building from collapsing when a lower floor suffers catastrophic damage. The images of both of these realities had seared themselves into my subconscious to the point where it decided to offer its two cents worth. As far as I am aware, this is the only skyscraper design to date that offers either structural redundancy or horizontal egress.

*later that evening*

The following was written to accompany my contribution to the HBO special A Tribute to Heroes:

"Dear Beautiful Souls,

My life can be measured in a series of two hour clips of intense experiences and their associated memories. One such clip is of the woman I love and I watching the sunset from the observation deck of the World Trade Center. Even now I can see her sitting beside me with her arms propped on the rail, gazing out the window at the lights coming up over Manhattan. She turns her head to face me and with the most brilliant smile you could ever hope to see, gives me an "I love you" that has echoed through my mind a thousand times since. Another clip is of the first two hours spent glued with stunned horror to live coverage of the attacks and the collapse of the towers. The image of the second jet is as equally indelible as my lover's smile. Another such clip is of last night watching a parade of beautiful souls displaying the best of their human spirit through the font of their talents.

The thing that made it so moving was that I had spent the previous week and a half cynically convincing myself of the ignorance and knee-jerk irresponsibility of our leaders, as I so often tend to do. I had begun to give up hope of our ability to pull ourselves through this tragedy and our pending struggle against terrorism. Last night I was able to spend two glorious hours reveling in the beauty of the human spirit as it was displayed in its full glory right before my eyes. And this time it was no isolated incident, nor a Spielberg movie merely depicting the glory of man. I was not sitting around a campfire listening to otherwise underrated musicians pouring their hearts into a song, I was watching the simulcast of a performance seen around the globe. I know your intent was to raise money, and I'm sure you did a fantastic job of that, but of far greater importance, you displayed to all of mankind the true beauty of the human soul.

God bless Julia Roberts for not crying during her address, as I was so tearfully begging her not to do. (The first tears I had been able to shed since the attacks.) God bless Neil Young for his genius and powerfully emblazoned spirit. God bless Tom Hanks for being the kind of man the rest of us should hope to be. God bless Sheryl Crow for being such a fully actuated human being. God bless Clint Eastwood for being Clint Eastwood. And God bless all of you for pulling off such an astonishing event. And yes, I noticed no one introduced themselves by name, amplifying the fact that this was not about a bunch of celebrities, but a group of fellow humans. It's so rare, and hence so unfortunate, that we get such chances to revel in one another's glory. Thank you for that brief opportunity last night. We should all hope to touch just one soul with even a fragment of the radiance with which you so lovingly touched mine."

*Monday September 24th 2001*

I've put Louie in storage in anticipation of leaving next Sunday for Manhattan for at least a week. So far the damage has been mostly images on a screen and will not seem real until I see it for myself. I had been struggling with the idea of walking off my consulting gig, when a funny thing happened: I got fired!

I told CL and her mother they simply didn't renew my contract, but it was more of a freak, serendipitous accident - although by now we all know better than that. I was working the other night and decided to leave a goofball voicemail for a colleague, making fun of her for calling in sick that day. The next morning there was a call from a very pissed off sounding man who turned out to be her boss's boss. Suffice to say the whole thing snowballed from there, with phone calls and emails circulating between Detroit, Boston, and Orlando, and by noon I was gone. The best part is the ex is out of town for the week so I hope to get in some serious dad time before I leave, although I'm not very high on CL's social calendar.

☙

Last week I heard a news story saying Congress had tried to pass tighter airport security restrictions almost ten years ago but the airline industry lobbied against it. Why have we come to accept this practice as a normal part of our political process? Why should campaign contributions outweigh what is right? Who lobbies for truth when no financial gain is involved? The goal of our leaders should be working to maintain the dictums set forth in the Preamble to our Constitution, not their own personal gain.

The other day I heard Giuliani saying the best way to honor the dead is to "go about our normal lives", which is only partly true. It is true that we should not allow these events to disrupt our lives any more than necessary, but it was our bovine adherence to "normal" that led us down this path in the first place.

So many simply go about the routine of what they think makes up a day: Wake, shower, coffee, commute, work, lunch, work, commute, drinks, dinner, "How was your day dear?", TV, more drinks, uh-uh um-um, and sleep. Only to wake up the next day to do it all over again, never stopping to check their motivations or ask themselves why.

CL and I were discussing this just the other day in terms of the structure of our current educational system as being merely the training grounds for the "wake up to go somewhere and do what other people tell you to do" mentality. We've all heard it a million times and have seen it spelled out in living color at the theàtre: It is only the heart that should be our primary motivation for what we do in life. But all too often it is the routine, or the pursuit of sex or status or power, or any distraction that will take our minds off the fact that we have completely forgotten the true meaning of passion.

There are a number of potentialities surrounding this trip, the most important being that my sainted grandmother, my Yoda, is in the hospital and will in all likelihood not be going home, which would mean my flying to Memphis for the funeral. And the architect in me needs to mourn the loss of two incredible examples of human achievement, which I hope to do at the site.

## Wednesday September 26th 2001

I've spent so much of my life wanting to be complete. For the longest time I thought I would not be complete without my Ideal. Then there is the ongoing quest for some elusive knowledge or meaning. Add to this a need for a purposeful life, passionate motivations, and a better physical engine with which to enjoy it all, and you get a life dedicated mostly to longing. A life dominated by disappointment and dissatisfaction. The only thing I hope for now is that I am finally ready to move beyond that phase of my life.

I know what it's like to want. I've known longing so consuming you would sell the blood in your veins to be fulfilled. Rare has been the exhilaration of such fulfillment, common the depression of want. A self-immolation akin to banging one's head against the proverbial wall, as if the life or love or job or respect or friends you imagine to be on the other side are somehow better than those same things you unknowingly reject on this side. The most dangerous tendency is to over-inflate the good you *do* find to the point of implosion. Then to rationalize the resultant devastation by compounding the delusion of disappointment and walking away from the experience convinced that life really is as dreadful as you've imagined. That true beauty is an elusive hoax, when all the while it was right before your eyes. Just as there are kernels of Truth to be found in all things, so too are there kernels of beauty as well, and passion and meaning and complete. Just as gathering kernels of Truth is the only path to Knowledge, so too is gathering these other kernels the only path to complete. Neither is to be found in any one thing, place, person or circumstance, but all are to be found everywhere you look. To disregard any portion is to forever remain un-whole.

*Sunday September 30th 2001,*
*Manhattan*

Have you ever scooped out a fireplace or poured water on a campfire or stuck your nose in a dirty ashtray? That's the first thing that strikes you when you step off the subway at Wall Street, the smell. Nineteen days after the attacks, in a light drizzling rain, four to five blocks from Ground Zero, and the burnt odor still lingers.

This is my first chance to let it all sink in, so my mind is still down there, while the rest of me has found sanctuary at the Rodeo Grill on 3rd and 27th. Part of me is feeling like I should bust loose with the incredible story of my very first encounter in the City, but having just walked past block after block of homemade missing person posters plastered on every vertical surface along the streets, I just can't work up the gumption. My hands feel like appended sandbags laying on the laptop, only grudgingly reaching for the keys after being coerced into each stroke. Luckily the music here sounds like Howling Wolf doing Dylan covers, or there would be no pace to this effort at all.

Usually when you see the face of a pretty girl in ads or magazines, you get a different feeling than when you see similar pictures with, "Last seen..." or "Worked in Tower One, 94th floor...", scribbled in Sharpie underneath. Smiling faces of a man in suit and tie as if at a family dinner celebrating a new promotion. A man in a jogging suit holding his son. A nameless face looking startled into the camera, as if a friend just had a good laugh from catching her off guard. All taped to individual 8-1/2 x 11 plain white sheets of paper, with handwritten descriptions and pleas for any information. Like something you might see on the bulletin board at your local supermarket imploring a runaway to come home, except there's row after row after row of them. It's hard to imagine that any one of these people may have been caught on camera plunging to their death or that their fingers and toes are now being referred to as body parts by the media. And I'm just some guy passing by on the street, I can't imagine what it must be like for the person who had to make the poster. Who had to sift through a box of otherwise pleasant memories to select the best and most recent facial shot. The folk artist in me was immediately struck with the staying power of a collage made from these posters, saved to recall the moment when so many people suddenly began to care all at once.

But tonight everything seems miserable, almost as if even the neon flashes not "come hither" but "remember". At the various memorials scattered at random around the neighborhoods, rain tatters the posters and wilts the flowers. Even the banners made by local school children, hand drawn flags and plenty of 'God Bless America's, are not spared. Tonight there is little distinction between the melancholy normally associated with a dreary, drizzly night on the streets and the somber reality of the City.

*Monday October 1st 2001*

I'm anxious to get to the site but I have to share yesterday's good news before I get all mellow again. Remember the various energy manifestation examples we've experienced along the way, like the good energy of Padre' versus the bad energy of Orlando? Well, get this... From the moment I walked in the front door of the hostel where I'm staying, I have been completely absorbed in positive energy. As it happened, the owner was working the desk when I got here and we spent an hour and a half talking about life and destiny and evolution and the power of the mind and all the stuff I love talking about. And he teaches the power of the mind to influence individual destiny! We got a little off course with evolution versus creation, but all in all it was a wonderful welcome. I can still see this 60 year old man's brilliant smile, the way his eyes lit up when he talked, and his animations. He said 25 years ago two of his younger brothers and their "wise" friends had him tied up in a boat with cinder blocks strapped to his feet, demanding

$150K ransom or they were going to "feed him to the fishes". He evidently had the whole "life flashes before your eyes" experience and has been on a quest for Truth ever since. It seems we have come to many similar conclusions.

> 8:40 AM... On the subway to Bowling Green, the stop at the southern tip of the restricted radius around the site.

The faces don't look much different than from before the attacks, and the conversations are all the same. Everyone's acting self-absorbed or wearing the guise of being okay. No budding intimacy to speak of. Once again I am equally as guilty of this as in the opening entry. I tell myself people just need some one person to make the first move, that now they are even more scared than usual.

CB

My first glimpse of damage was of the east face of one of the World Financial Center buildings adjacent to the site. A sheer glass wall of 40 floors with at least 15% of the panes broken. Then a stunned moment of trying to grasp reality, as if my memories of the World Trade Center are like the images of the perfect world I carry around inside my head, in that one is, or was, no more tangible than the other. The WTC stood as a glorious monument to the abilities of man. Already there is debate against going back with skyscrapers, but I believe I answered that a few entries back.

I discovered part of the reason for the lingering smell. In the daylight you can look up and clearly see all the window ledges in the area are still covered in soot and debris. I saw a lot of cleaning activity, but mostly restricted to sweeping the sidewalks and cleaning street level windows. There are a few intersections around the restricted perimeter where you can actually see the rubble, but for the most part it's surrounded by a continuous plywood and plastic barricade. I did see the actual remnants of one of the towers, but my brain refused to register this in connection with the soaring towers in my mental data bank filed under the heading "World Trade Center."

More than a block from the site a once exclusive jewelry store sits empty, its useless trinkets gone, hastily retrieved from a thick layer of dust and ash. There is little doubt this dust contains the cremated remains of those who will never be found. Ironically, perhaps even someone who before the attacks mistakenly felt there was something of value inside the now abandoned shop.

The last time I was at the WTC, Saint Jane and I were marveling at the tens of thousands of people scurrying below, each with their own lives, fears, and dreams. Now I'm sitting in a coffee shop just a couple of blocks north of the site, gazing out the window and thinking the same thing. One point the hostel owner and I shared yesterday was that on the inside we are all the same. But then he kept tried to say that healing has to start with governments and corporations. The flaw in this thinking is that it places the call for peace somewhere other than on the individual. As I've said many times, it is up to each and every one of us to ensure our own sense of inner peace and purpose. It is true that governments and corporations need to change, but this is not something we can expect to just magically happen. It is the *individuals* involved in these organizations who must change, and the individuals *not* involved in these organizations who must hold them to it.

*same day 5:26 PM*

Well, it's happened. My Yoda is gone. I got an email from OB saying she crossed over yesterday, so I'll be making a 24 hour round trip to Memphis tomorrow.

*Wednesday October 3rd 2001*

I'm not a big fan of open casket funerals, although this time I couldn't completely turn away. The one thing I focused on was how well they did her hands. I didn't want to think about the make-up, I just wanted to remember my grandmother's hands. My mother said that my grandmother had made the dress she was buried in. If I want anything of hers it's something she made, like this delicately crocheted bedspread in her guestroom. As it is, I made sure CL got a porcelain tea set that belonged to my grandmother's grandmother as a child.

We buried her in the oldest cemetery in the city, eight plots down from where she, as a 14 year old in 1919, buried her own father who had fallen victim to the Spanish flu. At the graveside ceremony my mother suggested that each of the four grandchildren say a few words. I was grateful for the opportunity and shared the story of our last visit.

*same day 4:47 PM*
*Washington Square Park*

Okay, so all joking and mystical allusions to destiny aside, I have to share something that seriously approaches the profound. A few years ago I had a dream about staying in some low rent accommodation in the City and having a conversation with a man in a pub, and his saying, "But you have to think if they were willing to give their lives for their cause, they must have believed in what they were doing." To which I responded, "But you are assuming their lives meant something to them." The thing I remember most about the dream is walking out of the pub and into my destiny. I have dreamt of destiny several times, and while I can't always remember what I was doing in the dream, I categorize the experience by the aura of the dream. Like the events were taking place on a dramatically over lit stage and every movement was slow and exaggerated, with a typical low hum symphonic soundtrack. Today as I was coming down the stairs at the hostel and glanced out the window at the back patio of the pub next door, I *knew* we had been there and that the topic was of course the suicide terrorists. I don't know when or if this will happen, or if it even needs to in order to have the same effect. One realization which has solidified on this adventure is the understanding that destiny is not some elusive future, but the seriousness with which we treat each and every passing moment. That destiny is not a place, or even any particular set of circumstances, but the attention we give to right now.

*Thursday October 4th 2001 10:43 AM,
NYC Library*

I don't believe in this sort of thing, but check out my horoscope from this week's Village Voice:

*"It's Soul Retrieval Week, Taurus. You will attract the help of divine and human allies alike, whenever you take measures to reclaim missing pieces of your soul. Are there relatives, either dead or alive, who stole some of your precious essence? Go into deep meditation and negotiate with them for its return. Have the betrayals of people you once trusted caused your beauty to dim? Fill your warrior heart with outrageous, courageous love and fight for the restitution of your lost gifts. Your hour of psychic unification is at hand."*

This makes me wonder about the relationship between déjà vu in terms of forecasting destiny and my assertions of yesterday that true destiny involves mindfully living the present. PF once said that experiences of déjà vu are our future selves tapping us on the shoulder alerting us to future events, or guiding us along so to speak. It may be the spirits of our deceased loved ones showing an insightful prediction of things to come, in hopes we will take notice and change our course if necessary. The same can be said of dreams. In either case it remains an important part of living a connected and healthy life to be as attentive as possible to these subtle hints.

How do I feel about dealing with my family or ex-friends in terms of reclaiming missing pieces of my soul? I have learned to regenerate my soul by meditating on a leaf or the bubbling water of a fountain. As much as I would love to resolve past ills, I can only focus on those phenomena over which I have some semblance of control. The Universe will deal with each of us in turn. I have to maintain faith that the Universe will give me everything I need, including any lost pieces of my soul.

*Friday October 5th 11:10 PM,
Esperanto Café in the Village*

In a city of 7M people, sitting on a plush red couch next to two beautiful women, yet still I am alone. Walking the streets I see glimpses of past loves in almost every face. Speaking of which, have I told you about the most beautiful night of my life?

From the moment I met Saint Jane I was desperately in love, although I was fairly certain she had no clue. As fate would have it, we had an opportunity to spend a few days together out of town, strictly as friends, part of which included spending the night at another friend's house. I explained that my friend had mistakenly assumed we were lovers and planned for she and I to sleep in his bed in his efficiency apartment, while he camped out on the floor. Much to my amazement, she said she felt our friendship was strong enough to platonically share a bed. So there we were, having a pleasant conversation while driving to my friend's house, when she says, "You know, I think I'm really developing a major crush on you." I was completely floored and had no idea what to say. I can remember the anticipation of that night as we were getting ready for bed. Of her brushing her teeth and putting on skin tight sweat pants to sleep in. There are few moments in your life as ecstatic as the first time the woman you love slips under the covers with you. I gave her a pleasant "Good night" and was lying on my side of the bed as nervous as a virgin after the prom. I had no idea what to do or say or how to act, when all of a sudden she pulled herself against me and kissed me ever so lightly just below my left ear. Even now I can feel it. I spent the next few hours, in full bed clothes, with this phenomenal woman in my arms. Every breath of that night is like a complete love story unto itself, captured forever in my soul. I would trade the bulk of every sexual experience of my life just to relive the beauty, intensity, and innocent tenderness of that night.

*Saturday October 6th 2001 11:32 AM*

I've caught myself questioning destiny. Like expecting something to happen if I just miss a train or if the doors mysteriously reopen as I approach. I find myself saying, "Okay, I saw that, now what?" Then I get a little depressed when nothing happens. Or you make plans and are lost for a comeback when they fall through. Last night I went to an Internet café in Times Square, only to discover it was closed due to connection trouble. So I spent the next 2 1/2 hours wandering the streets of the Village waiting to feel the new ripple. At one point I remember doing a James Dean, waiting for Saint Jane to magically appear on the opposite corner. Needless to say, no such miracles. Just a lonely, deranged, rebel wannabe, leaning against a lamp post smoking a Camel Light.

*Sunday October 7th 2001 7:14 PM*

We started bombing today.

Let me share a few quips from two incredible conversations I had in the hostel kitchen this morning...

A molecular biology student from Jamaica, who was only at the hostel because she had stayed late volunteering at Bellevue Hospital the night before, was telling me about the economic situation in her country. It seems that Dole (the company) "successfully lobbied against" importing bananas from Jamaica, which caused a complete collapse of the local independent farmer's livelihood. Now they are raping the countryside for timber and anything else they can find for export. As a result, they currently have the highest rate of deforestation on the planet. How's that for mindlessly following a dollar?

Then I met this incredible guy from England who shared, unbeknownst to himself, the root premise of Unification Theory - that "billboard" vision from Book III. Namely that our only hope is to meld Eastern and Western tradition into a more cohesive strategy for the survival of mankind. He termed it "essence vs. existence". What we were trying to figure out was how to go about the business of earning a living without sacrificing personal passion. But then he went on to say something that floored me in terms of its relevance. He said that man was fundamentally okay, just asleep. And that when we awake, the next step will be to admit to, and deal with, the following three facts: A. We didn't want to awake. B. It was ourselves keeping us asleep. and C. The capacity to awaken was inside us the entire time.

Unbelievable.

*Tuesday October 9th 2001 3:28 PM*

I am sitting at one of my favorite spots on Earth, the traffic island in the middle of Times Square. The police have it barricaded from side to side so it's nowhere near as crowded as usual. I have decided to sit here and write until the cops run me off or the laptop battery dies, whichever comes first.

One of the things I like to do is feel energy. Sitting here, with the traffic coming at me on both sides, is like being the coiled magnet in the center of an electric generator. There is so much activity and lights and people and accumulated spirits from decades gone by, it feels like if I rubbed my hands together sparks would fly out of my ears and my hair would stand up straight. If I knew I were destined to get struck by lightning I would sit right here until it happened, because that would be a fitting climax to what I feel. I only wish people could see the life and dreams and ingenuity and sweat that went into the making of this place. Plus I know there are trains running beneath me and planes flying overhead. I can look up, above the billboards and skyscrapers, and imagine orbiting satellites and the little white doughboys dangling outside the space station. Never in my wildest dreams could I imagine that on the opposite side of the world the events that could erupt any day into the conflict to end all conflicts are now taking place.

When I see the world as I wish it were, I see bright eyes and radiant smiles, clean streets and clean air. No one with the droop of death to their face or plod of dread to their step. No one wants to escape because everyone is ecstatic to be here. No more waiting for the grave for our reward, we claim it with each waking breath. I see you coming towards me down the street, and while I may not know your name, you are not a stranger. I know if I wanted to hug you or share a kind word, these would both be welcome.

*Tuesday October 16th 2001 6:15 AM,
back in Florida*

For some reason I've long since given up trying to understand, I'm just not all that great at dealing directly with people. Assuming you've made it this far, I really do hope you were able to get something out of this effort. To be honest, I never wanted to live to see the day our future as a species was in question. I was perfectly content with running around like Chicken Little complaining about it. Now that we are here, I find myself just as scared and confused as I imagine everyone else must be. I would love to spend my days sitting under a tree meditating on world peace, but we all know I'm just not there yet. I do continue to feel very strongly about MegaCity and the positive potentials for humanity's future. I know it sounds Utopian, but attempted Utopian societies of the past have only failed because not everyone involved wanted them to succeed. While I pray we never all think and act alike, we can certainly move away from unhealthy ways of thinking and acting. We are cognitive beings, and the only way we are going to survive is if more of us - all of us - start acting like it.

*Friday October 19th 2001 6:32 AM,
Fritz's Restaurant in Clearwater FLA*

Last night I had the most astounding series of dreams. The first part of the dream was of me as a kid training with a group of other kids for this insane bicycle obstacle course. I can remember parts where we had to cross paths in mid-air, with instant switch-backs and just about every sort of crazy maneuver you can think of. The training was great, but once we started our actual run everything started falling apart. Either our competition screwed us up or we crossed one path too many or something. To make matters worse, there was no longer any sort of trail markers to tell us how the race was organized. My only guide was this very real tugging sensation in my gut that told me where to go and when to turn. In the climatic leg of the race, I was peddling up a 45 degree hill with built-in wooden steps that threw the front wheel of my bike vertical with every other pedal stroke.

When I got to the top of the hill I found myself on a grass covered plateau, with a ring of friends and family standing around the perimeter cheering for me. I knew I was in "my place", an elusive and mostly imaginary spot where everything about myself and my life are incredible. I know when I'm in my place by the euphoric feeling that overwhelms me.

There is a level of joy so consuming that it has become entirely unimaginable to most people. Over the centuries this feeling has been romanticized as something only attainable through some sort of mystic process. One common name for it is nirvana, a level of bliss so tangible as to almost seem real. A state of mind where all concern for earthly matters completely falls away. It's as if there were nothing in the Universe except this inexplicable collection of thought energy you loosely recognize as yourself and the blazing heat of the sun, which surprisingly doesn't burn as you're swimming through it. In the dream I was so ecstatic that I broke down sobbing and fell to my knees. I was on all fours digging my fingers into the dirt when someone put their hand on my shoulder and asked if I was okay. All I managed to say was that I was so unbelievably happy I couldn't stand it.

The person who asked about me was my Ideal. I could see her face, but it wasn't Saint Jane. Then she said she wanted to introduce me to my spirit guide. We approached a man wearing a stereotypical brown monk's robe. There was a handful of people standing close to him as if around a cherished teacher. When he raised his face, the first thing I noticed was that his beard looked like one of those rugs made from different colored strips of fabric tied in knots and sewn together. The second thing I noticed was that the man was my brother, DAB. He had the most piercing gray eyes I've ever seen. We just gave each other an "I knew it all along" loving gaze and both went back to the dream.

I know I woke up intermittently during the dream, pressing the pillow to my face, tossing and turning and breathing like during sex. The euphoria was with me even awake. I remember mumbling "Oh my god" over and over and forcing myself immediately back to sleep.

When I first awoke this morning, I realized the meaning of the first part of the dream was that no matter what you expect of life, or what you have trained for, you always have to be ready to improvise on the fly. You have to take whatever comes your way and run with it. And sometimes you have to push yourself beyond what you think you're able to endure. Another realization was that there's not always going to be clear signs along the way. That even when it may not seem entirely logical to anyone else, you have to trust your own instincts and follow the tugging sensation in your own gut.

The most important part of last night's experience was a tiny taste of what I've always known was out there. A level of euphoria not induced by any drug, but always attainable at the deepest, most untainted core of our soul. For a few minutes after I awoke I remained in full dream mode, ready to take on life with my newfound certainties. But then, as I left the lot where I had parked the truck to sleep for the night, my first experience of my fellow man was of some guy in a pick-up tailgating me, honking and flashing his high beams. Here it was 6:15 in the morning, I was less than two minutes into consciousness, trying desperately to cling to a beautiful dream, and this jackass was acting like a cabbie in rush hour traffic.

It's sad, but even as I try to share this incredible story, I am confronted with the enemy sitting across from me in the diner. People who somehow manage to function, even though every action seems painful. As if every breath were drawn against the secret wish it were their last. These people not only loath their own existence, but fight against every notion of real joy they see in others. Trust me on this one, our real enemies are not in some desert on the other side of the globe, but walking our own streets. Those who long for the peace of the grave will never bring joy to life, either to yours, mine, or their own. Their only elation is for those things that in their twisted minds prove the imperfections of man and the fruitlessness of our existence.

It makes me so sick that I can't even talk about it anymore.

In the last few months I have gone from high-horse to gutter and back. I have faced two situations that should have cast me full-fledged onto my Path: JR hooked on crack and the terrorist attacks. In both instances the full reality of the situation was with me for a week or so, then receded back to something less than pure motivation. If you add to these experiences the things I've learned on the road and the tools handed to me like in last night's dream, I should not only be on my Path, but floating along in at least some recognizable state of nirvana. Whenever I have access to a mirror and am confronted with the "T-A-H-C-D" tattoo on my chest, I am reminded of the fact that I do not always live by this dictum. Someday I will face the accumulated destiny created by my thoughts of today, even those I should know better than indulging. I watch the sunset over the Gulf and try to focus on my own well-being, all the while knowing something is missing, that I am still somehow lacking.

I've decided, yet again, that all I can do is end this particular exercise. All any of us can ever do is keep on keeping on. It is true we must monitor every step and do the best we can in each instance, but the trick is simply to do. I know I've painted myself as someone you could easily call a naïve, self-absorbed hypocrite. I know I've gone way off in left field at times and waxed painfully obvious at others. But I also know I've enjoyed having you along for the ride.

I have come to accept the fact that if I were to wait until I were the person I imagine before sharing the things I have tried to share, I would never share them. That Knowledge is not only the commodity of sages, but within us all. That as painful or embarrassing as it may be at times, the best we can do for one another is to cleave our souls and share the good and the bad. That the only way to heal is to expose the wounds. That to deny pain is to amplify pain. That the tiny ills we all carry inside are compiling exponentially to create an ever growing sickness for humanity. That the only cure for humanity as a whole is to cure the individual. That the god we are waiting to pull the strings is slumbering peacefully, snuggled way down deep in our souls. That the pain and suffering will vanish, not in the grave, but the moment we nuzzle our own god. That your god is not my god, though they are the same God. That the world as we know it is the world we have created. And that in the end, we will all get what we deserve.

I only hope it isn't too late.

# ❧ Book VI ❧

*May 2020*

An entire generation has been thrust upon the planet and reached the age of majority since I was given that brief glimpse behind the curtain 18-1/2 years ago. That generation has known nothing but a perpetual state of undeclared war.

When I first started this journey I said, "I see two potential futures for humanity, both of which will be determined by our actions of today and irrevocably set over the next 20 years", then later added, "I see the next 20 years of our shared existence as being crucial to the next 200."

Those twenty years have now come and gone. As I write, we are in the midst of the very calamity I foresaw two decades ago. Not the pandemic per se', as much as the underlying social, political, and economic weaknesses it is revealing. And make no mistake, the manner in which we resolve these issues will have a direct and lasting impact for many generations to come.

If the spread of the virus shows us anything, it is confirmation of how intertwined the human family has become and how quickly the impact of our actions reverberates around the globe. It was the accumulated consequences of our collective short-sightedness that got us into this situation in the first place. And unless the pandemic effects real, positive change on a global scale, our struggles as a species are far from over. We will either choose to embrace the evolutionary profundity that has brought us this far, or we will, by default, continue to suffer every indignity wrought by our contrived ignorance.

It took from the end of the last Ice Age to the year 1800 (a period of roughly 12,000 years), for the global population to reach one billion. The next milestone of two billion was reached a mere **125 *years*** later. By the time I came along in 1963, the global population was just over 3.2 billion and has more than doubled in my lifetime. In the first 20 years of the 21st Century alone, we have *added* more human beings to the planet than were alive at the time of the American Revolution.

When you consider that the vast majority of our religious beliefs, political ideologies, and economic systems, are rooted in the era *before* our ecosystem was so overburdened, then you begin to grasp the urgent need for new solutions. Solutions that not only address exponential population growth and finite resources, but also how we can best ensure that *all* humans have the opportunity to enjoy their God-given right to a meaningful existence.

One of the most disheartening discoveries I made on my adventure was the realization that, compared to what life *could* be like if society functioned anywhere close to its true potential, *we* are the ones living in the dystopian future of science fiction. This to the point where it has become nearly impossible for any of us to avoid having some form of negative impact on the world around us. The insanity has gone on long enough. It is time to stop the mad dash before we all go over the edge of the abyss. We have the power within us to do so, the only question is will use it?

The best way to begin the healing process would be to set aside sentiment and suspicion and work as directly as possible with objective reality.

Objective reality is that which exists, and would continue to exist, with or without our comprehension of it. This reality is subject to the laws of physics and of nature. We, our physical beings, are a part of this reality. The manner in which we, our cognitive beings, comprehend this reality is unique to each of us, based on our respective physiological and psychological make up. Further still, what we see of the outside world is also largely determined by what we have been *conditioned* to see of the outside world. Nature *and* nurture.

Society is an ever-evolving attempt at finding the balance between our respective capacities to discern objective reality and the laws that govern that reality. Just as individuals suffer whenever attempting to exist outside these laws, so too does a society. Participating in a social fabric calls for each individual to extend their own capacity for discerning objective reality, to include gauging other individual's respective abilities to do the same, then deciding to either engage or avoid those individuals based on that ability. It's only natural that we should want to congregate in groups of likeminded people - those whose subjective realities are sufficiently similar to our own so as to coexist with minimal conflict - which has become known as the herd mentality. This is all well and good, except when any particular herd mindset attempts to circumvent the laws that govern the objective reality of the group.

This pandemic is simply nature's way of reminding us that despite whatever our cognitive beings may prefer to think, ultimately our physical beings are subject to laws beyond our control. Now is not the time to be guided by herd mentality. Now is not the time to risk your life based on the limitations of someone else's capacity, or lack thereof, to discern objective reality.

Now is the time to stop, take a deep breath, and trust your *own* gut. Even if it means rethinking everything you have been conditioned to believe about the world and your place in it. No aspect of our existence is above the laws of physics or of nature. I pray, as we all continue to work through this dire, global situation, that we allow nature to nudge us closer into alignment with these laws without too much fuss. Because the more we fight it, or the more we try to pretend we are above it, the worse it's going to be.

And for a real world demonstration of this, you need look no further than Donald Trump.

Never in my wildest dreams could I have imagined such a soulless, human'esque creature as Donald Trump occupying the White House. In the Introduction, which was written in that tiny apartment on South Padre', when I was going on about "The shallow bastard who has attached so much of his self-image to the dead protein cells sprouting off the top of his hollow skull", I wasn't specifically thinking about Trump. Those were the heady days before any of us *had* to think about Trump.

Trump is the embodiment of every negative human attribute I have decried this entire exercise. The evolutionary equivalent of the Neanderthal that scoffed at the first of his kind who dared to leave the cave. A vacuous effigy of a man, who would be a nonentity if left to his own devices. But since we worship both wealth and celebrity, he somehow managed to finagle himself into the most powerful office on the planet.

And to hell with his supposed politics. I'm not talking about politics. I can respect anyone's opinion who actually believes what they espouse and can back it up with intelligent dialogue. But anyone who has ever even slept through PSYCH101 can see that Trump doesn't actually *believe* anything, right, wrong, or indifferent. He lacks sufficient character to actually commit to any belief system, including political ideology.

Trump is both the canary **and** the methane in the coal mine for America. Not only does the fact of his election point to a disjointed political process that must be corrected post haste, but many, including myself, consider Trump to be the single greatest threat to our democracy. What more efficient way to sink a ship than for the captain himself to intentionally ram it into an iceberg?

Not only is Trump completely oblivious of the concept of introspection, but anything even remotely akin to such is in fact his greatest fear. Subconsciously he knows were he to ever look inside, all he would find is a dark empty shell. And any creature as fragile as Donald Trump would rather see the whole world go up in flames than ever admit he is wrong.

I pray it doesn't come to that. I pray this is the lowest we ever sink as a nation, that the Trump presidency is the brick wall of reality that provides both the final separation from the shortcomings of our past and the base from which to propel ourselves into a future that surpasses even our highest achievements to date.

CS

I cannot detail the roadmap of how we get from *this* reality to either the Millennium Tower or MegaCity phases of our future, but I have a very good idea of the initial step that will point us in the right direction.

I know there are bright and glorious days ahead for humanity, but we're not going to get there until we free our children from the burden of carrying our past mistakes. No longer can we afford to cram our frailties down the throats of our offspring, only to complain when they don't toe the line. No longer can we afford to cast one child into the gutter and another into a penthouse, then wonder in feigned astonishment at why one fails and the other succeeds.

It was Thomas More who, a full five centuries ago, first popularized this philosophy. Five hundred years and we still have not made any real effort to apply this supremely rational practice to the real world.

If our species is ever to reach our true potential, we must immediately adopt each and every social norm necessary to ensure better lives for our progeny. We can no longer cast them into situations where they are forced to struggle for their basic needs, or cause them to spend their entire adult lives working to overcome the impact of negative circumstances endured as children. Simply provide them the nurturing and support every infant needs, then allow their innate human intellect and empathy to develop naturally. Give them love and let them grow.

There's no need to concoct a list of what *to* teach our children, as long as we can agree on what *not* to teach our children. Give them the basic facts, free of bias and bigotry, and let them take it from there. And we don't have to try and provide all the solutions either. Once we stop passing on the problems, the solutions will naturally take care of themselves.

We don't have to teach our children *what* to think or even *how* to think, as long as we teach them *to* think.

As for the present generations, we still have a tremendous untapped resource to rely upon. Do you remember at the end of Book III, when I asked you to gauge your internal balance of love versus loathing? At the time, I referred to this as your level of "give-a-damn", but have since learned this is an emerging field of study called Love Quotient, or LQ.

I prefer to think of the global average LQ in the same way climatologists think of the global average temperature. Laymen hear talk of a 2-3 degree rise in global temperature and wonder how a seemingly insignificant change could have such a tremendous impact on the environment. The same is true of the global average LQ. The slightest tilt one way or the other has social implications on a scale nearly impossible to fathom.

A society can only thrive if its mean LQ tilts towards love, will continue to exist for only as long as its mean LQ is at least neutral, and starts to fail the moment its mean LQ leans towards loathing.

Right now humanity is in a bit of an LQ lull. But, like the environment, if we act quickly enough, there is still time to tilt back towards love and get society back on track. Imagine what life would be like if we all cared enough to pull just a tiny bit harder in the right direction. Not click our heels and magically poof into a fully actuated existence, but at least try to stop stumbling backwards.

The reason I hold out hope for our future is because I have *seen* our future. Maybe it's Millennium Tower that is 200 years hence and MegaCity a couple hundred years after that. Either way, I do not see us struggling through an apocalyptic dystopia, fighting for our lives against diabolical machines or brain eating zombies. If these had been my visions, I would have jumped ship a long time ago.

☙

I'm sure it was obvious to others, although I only figured it out halfway through editing this edition, that the audience I was speaking to the entire time was myself. The me I am now. My older, slightly more cynical self who needed to hear the words of my younger, more hopeful self. Even though it's a bit preachy, I still managed to say then what I needed someone to remind me of now, that humans are strong, resilient, and capable, and that everything we need is already inside us.

I also needed the admonitions imploring myself to do more, to try harder, and to live more passionately. I grew up watching my father robotically go through the motions of his day: Get up with the five o'clock alarm to go to a job that required little mental effort and even less passion, only to come home to watch TV and go to bed. I hated everything about that life and wanted anything *but* that for my own.

I didn't become an architect because I was good at it, I became an architect because it wasn't blue collar. I *became* good at it, the technical aspects anyway, because I was raised blue collar.

Going into it, I already understood the basic mechanics of architecture, the physical realities of placing one block on top of another to form a structure.

In the years since the close of Book V, I have focused on turning deeper within to more fully embrace the ideas I was only beginning to comprehend when we first started this journey so long ago. And just like the boy on the bicycle in the dream, I have learned to trust and go with my gut without hesitation. Even when no one else around me gets it, even when I don't get it, I try to follow my instincts with as little interference from my more malleable conscious self as I can manage. This of course means a bit of asphalt still gets stuck in the teeth from time to time, but even these occasions are counted as learning experiences.

Each day I am confronted by how much I still do not know. My "philosophies", if you choose to call them that, are not based on an understanding of, or comparison to, the thoughts of those who have come before. To me, philosophy isn't about deep ponderings and verbose dialogue, but about whatever makes you get out of bed in the morning. Philosophy is however you choose to view the day to day realities of life within the broader context the overall experiential journey.

Becoming your better self is a lifelong process. A combination of raw introspection, coupled with constantly minding the wake you leave behind and always taking responsibility for your actions. Of not only surrounding yourself with people you respect and admire, but also with those you can trust to be honest, objective mirrors.

And yes, even accepting the fact that sometimes life really is about getting up when you need to get up, so you can go where you need to go, and do what needs to be done.

But if you make no attempt to at least *pursue* your better self, you are doomed to little more than repeating the same life over and over for the rest of your days. A life for which the conditions were set by random coincidence of birth and the parameters prescribed to you when you were just a hungry little sponge.

Becoming your *better* self means recognizing you will never be your *best* self, as there is no such thing. No matter how much potential you embrace, no matter how much you accomplish, no matter what skills you acquire or experiences you enjoy or fulfillment you realize, there is always going to be more. And *that* is what makes life such a wonderous experience. Not the berating ourselves for what we haven't done, or chiding ourselves for what we should be doing, but realizing this adventure is literally boundless.

A world without end, Amen.

૭૩

Before I close, I want to update you on a few of the other characters introduced along the way, which I will try to do in the order they appeared in the book.

Both parents are gone. They were in a serious auto accident on their way home from Jonesboro on Easter Sunday 2008. My dad had to be airlifted to the Med, my mother was transported by ambulance. Although my mother's injuries were not as severe, her already compromised states of health - both mental and physical - meant she couldn't muster the gumption to pull through. She crossed over that Wednesday. It took a full two months for my dad to recover from his injuries, then we lost him two years later to melanoma.

I was living and working in Manhattan at the time of the accident but packed up and came home overnight. At least I can look back and rightfully claim I reached what any architect would call the pinnacle of their career: Working on honest-to-god skyscrapers in the greatest city on Earth.

I have since been living back in my old neighborhood, which, in the thirty-five years since I first moved away, morphed from being a close-minded, working class neighborhood in an advanced state of decline, into a super-inclusive, culturally diverse neighborhood that now ranks as one of the top ten in the country. I recently purchased a two-story commercial building situated halfway between an old theater where my parents dated as teenagers and the former A&P where my sainted grandmother taught me how to shop as a kid. We are in the process of transforming it into what I call a "creative collaborative" shared environment, which not only means I get to surround myself with beautiful souls, but also that I can finally fulfill my dream of having enough space to work on multiple projects simultaneously.

Louie is currently sitting 30 feet over my shoulder out in the driveway, patiently waiting for the frame-off restoration that may or may not ever come. I've rebuilt much of the drivetrain, now it's the body in need of attention. We wound up traveling all over the east coast, from Mexico to Canada together. Every time I climb in the cab for his weekly maintenance crank, the memories of our time on the road together come pleasantly flooding back.

I finally found my high school sweetheart, right where her mother said I would. She was working Summer Avenue near Hollywood and looked exactly like what up to that moment any of us would have called a crack whore. I don't use that particular phrase anymore, especially the whore part. It was as horrifying an experience as you can imagine. I couldn't tell what stage of the crack roller coaster she was on but she was clinching a half pint of rotgut in her hand. Even through the fog of this nightmare she still recognized me.

We rode around and talked for a few minutes but in the end I had no idea of what else to do other than drop her back off where I found her. Sometime around 2007 she was found dead, lying face down in someone's front yard. If God ever granted me three wishes, one would be for her to have never taken her first step down that path.

It took a solid decade to get over Saint Jane, at least to the extent one does get over such things. Our time together was short-lived but had a profound impact on my life nonetheless. I've long had another book idea in mind, *Love Letters to an Unknown Ideal*, in which I hope to further explore my personal evolution in the ways of love. In the meantime, I'm thankful to be in a loving, incredibly supportive, long-term relationship with an extraordinary human, who seems to feel the same about me.

My daughter is doing great and has since had a daughter of her own. It's hard to believe that CL is almost the same age I was when I started this adventure. I can't even begin to describe what an incredible mother she is and how proud I am of her. At eleven, my granddaughter is light years beyond where I was at her age.

I did eventually make it to the Grand Canyon. Twice, actually. The first was in the summer of 2005. I was living in Upstate New York at the time, and took the Amtrak cross country to Winslow, Arizona. My friend Padre' Fred, who in the interim had moved to Holbrook, played chauffeur from there. Then in the summer of 2007, I took a two week solo road trip in a half-length school bus I had converted into a camper. I know after a week of camping on the South Rim I was approaching Zen Master mode (who wouldn't), but I can't recall any specific visions. Of course, visions aren't like that anyway.

My nephew is still one of the finest men I know. He is now married and raising a beautiful family of his own in Texas.

My middle brother crossed over in early 2008. His body simply decided it had had enough abuse and began systematically shutting down. I was walking around the Upper West Side when the end finally came and can clearly remember the wave of anger that washed over me as his energy dissipated. The house where he was living at the time, the house our dad grew up in, is now my forever home.

My oldest brother crossed over in October of 2002. Thankfully he was home in bed and just didn't wake up one Saturday morning. For such a troubled soul, he apparently touched many lives. Visitation at the funeral home was from 6:00-9:00, and at 10:00 the line to pay respects was still out the door. I wish I had known *that* man better.

My dad and I managed to reconcile our relationship after JR's passing. It was almost as if he said to himself, "I guess my sons aren't going to live forever, maybe I should try to get to know them." But as I mentioned in Book IV, there was also some maturing there on my part too. Whatever the case, our last few years together were remarkably mellow.

I never had the opportunity for such reconciliation with my mother.

I wasn't going to mention my sister. I had written an update blurb for her earlier but then made the conscious decision to delete it. I am only sitting here now, on the very morning I had intended to upload the final text for publication, adding the following paragraphs because Tom Hanks shifted his gaze half a degree and stared at me through the TV screen last night.

My sister and I suffered a major falling out in the aftermath of our parents' accident. There's no reason to rehash the painful details here, but suffice it to say that more than a decade later, my bitterness towards her is still sufficient enough to make me want to pretend she is not a part of my story.

I am not who I am because I found some great and powerful strength within myself to heal, that strength is embedded deep in the human genome we all share. I am who I am because my sister shielded my Inner Child long enough for him to gain a footing. If not for my sister, I would have wound up in a very similar boat as she and my two brothers. It was my sister who shielded me from our mother's demented wrath and provided the love and nurturing our mother failed to give them, that Georgia Tann failed to give her, that god-only-knows who failed to give Georgia Tann.

All of these people made me who I am. Good, bad, or indifferent, each had a profound and everlasting impact on my life. And for that, I am eternally grateful.

◌

Once the mechanisms were in place to start rebuilding at the World Trade Center site, I developed a modest presentation of the conceptual skyscraper from Book V as my official response to their RFQ. Of course, being a request for *qualifications*, I was tossed out in the first round. Regardless of whatever advanced safety features the concept would have introduced, as a standalone, unproven architect, I was nowhere near qualified.

# MILLENNIUM TOWER

35 Floors at 40,000 s.f. each = 1,400,000 s.f.

36 Floors at 80,000 s.f. each = 2,880,000 s.f.

124 Floors Totaling 2100'

Concrete shear walls articulated at exterior

51 Floors at 150,000 s.f. each = 7,650,000 s.f.

Primary structural grid articulated at exterior

World Trade Center Memorial Garden

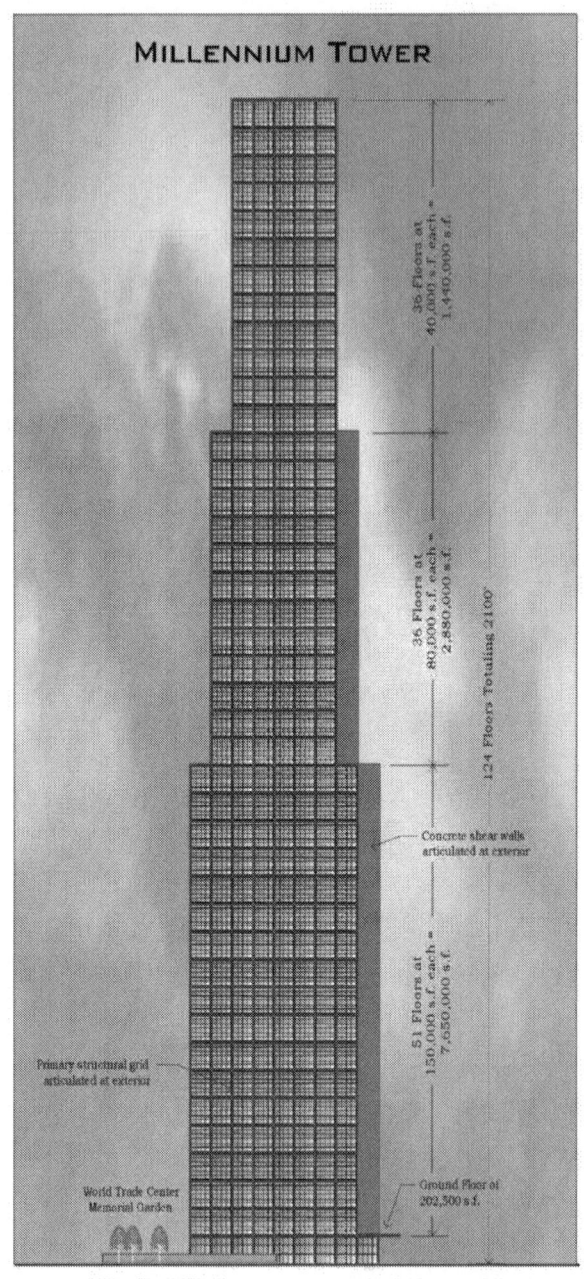

Ground Floor at 202,500 s.f.

**TOTAL AREA:**
**12,172,500 S.F.**
(NOT INCLUDING INTERIOR CORE)

**ELEVATION**
SCALE: 1" = 250'-0"

All designs, structural innovations and proprietary details, are protected under
copyright #VAu 530-067, issued September 26th 2001 - Aaron James

I did however, get to help design and build a WTC memorial in Malone, New York, which consists mainly of a cast concrete scaled model of the buildings and a commemorative plaque. Since I sponsored the plaque, I took it upon myself to pen the tribute:

**September 11th 2001**
**The finest achievements of man, which**
**took decades to conceive and construct,**
**were brought down in a matter of hours.**

**Let us never fail to reverently ponder**
**the vast gulf between the glorious**
**existence we are capable of living, and**
**the horrific reality we are often**
**called to endure. For it is only in**
**diligent pursuit of the former that we**
**realize the latter need never be.**

ଔ

I want to close with a few words to our future generations, a gentle reminder that if we are ever to reach our true potential as a species, it will not be through war but through peace. The text comes from a speech I was fortunate enough to give in January of 2002. You may recall the title from Book III.

# Unification Theory

From our very emergence as a species, we have been separating as a people. This separation has been driven by a fear of that *other* tribe, that other race, or other nation. Over time, we evolved separate skin tones and physical characteristics, as well as separate cultures, religions, and political ideologies. The final consequence of this separation is the fact that now we don't even know the person living next door, much less on the other side of town. The faces we meet in the grocery store, and even in our own beds, for the most part remain strangers.

Yet today, we face the future of humanity not as individuals, but as one. Today we are faced with the ultimate reality that we will either intentionally seek to reunify as a global family, or we will self-destruct, of our own neglect and by our own hand.

But there is hope. The one fact which has remained constant over the millennia is that on the inside we are all the same. We all crave peace and the freedom to pursue a passionate and meaningful existence. No longer can we afford to divide along *any* lines, be they racial, religious, national, or otherwise. We must band together against the root cause of *all* atrocities, which is the fear and despair that torments a person when they languish without peace in their soul.

We must stop deifying greed and a lust for domination as aspects of the powerful and recognize them for precisely what they are: The flailing, misguided efforts of the weak. For it is only the weak who try to dominate others and only the weak who horde material gain without concern for the welfare of others.

Atrocities are initiated by a very few, but are perpetuated by each and every one of us who simply go about the rote actions of our day without a specific desire to strive for peace. Yet all we need do is heed this natural law: Where there is no light, there is darkness.

Light is the measurable, darkness is merely a void. Light is the positive, darkness is literally that which does not exist. For there is only light and the absence of light. Good and the absence of good. Peace and the absence of peace.

By the absolute promotion of peace, the brutal realities that have long seemed so concrete, will simply vanish back into the void from whence they came. Not by mandate or force, but by the simple fact that they are not a natural part of our existence. Social justice, economic stability, and an ecological balance that supports *all* life, will only come as a manifestation of peace. There is no government or religion that will save us. We have to save ourselves.

It is time for each and every one of us to make our voices heard, to make every single action of every single day stand for what we believe. We must release our individual fears, wants, and agendas, and work ceaselessly to cultivate the common bonds we all share. Let us commit today to the task of promoting peace. Peace at the core of our being and peace in every action and interaction.

For the remainder of our days, we must all continuously strive for global reunification through peace.

Made in the USA
San Bernardino, CA
09 June 2020